Jesus
AND THE
12 STEPS

THE BIBLICAL RESPONSE TO ADDICTION
IS NOT WHAT YOU THOUGHT

Jesus and the 12 Steps

The Biblical Response to Addiction Is Not What You Thought

Mark Denison D.Min.

Published by Austin Brothers Publishing,

Fort Worth, Texas

www.abpbooks.com

ISBN 978-1-7333130-1-8

Library of Congress Control Number:2019915828

Cover design by Laurie Barboza - Design Stash Books

(DesignStashBooks@gmail.com)

Printed in the United States of America

2019 -- First Edition

AUSTIN
BROTHERS PUBLISHING

PERSONAL ENDORSEMENTS

Jesus and the 12 Steps is a unique book in that it uses well-known stories from Scripture to make the steps of recovery come alive. Dr. Denison is succinct and to the point, allowing the reader to absorb the message without getting bogged down with endless excursions into theology. This book is essential to Christians whose preconceived notions might cause them to be reluctant to work the 12 Steps.

Dr. Milton Magness
Founder of Hope & Freedom
Author, Stop Sex Addiction Now

Historians trace the founding of Alcoholics Anonymous and the Twelve Steps to the 1930s. But Mark Denison identifies their true origin – A.D. 30. This is an intriguing, well-written and profoundly insightful book. As I read Denison's skillfully illustrated 12 Steps in the ministry of Jesus, I kept asking myself, "Why didn't I see this before?"

David Murrow
Founder of Church for Men
Author, Why Men Hate Going to Church

Jesus and the 12 Steps can help you discover Jesus as your Higher Power even if you don't accept the modern trappings of religion. Mark writes not as a detached observer but with the wisdom of an experienced guide. Mark and his ministry have helped me. Jesus and the 12 Steps will help you, too.

Martin W.
Houston, Texas

It is a blessing to read anything from Mark Denison. In his latest book, Mark brings together the spiritual principles of the 12-Step program with the life and teaching of Jesus. There is no greater battle facing men today than the battle for sexual purity. Jesus is on our side in this fight and this book will help us follow his leading through the 12 Steps to help us win that battle.

Drew Chapados
Pastor – Westside Church of Christ
Windsor, Ontario, Canada

I have known Mark for 40 years. I applaud his ministry, There's Still Hope, as it leads men and women from the bondage of sex and porn addiction. His latest book is my favorite. *Jesus and the 12 Steps* offers concrete steps to healing, based on the proven 12-Step model and rooted in real life examples from the life of Christ.

Dr. Gary Wofford
Panama City Beach, Florida

Mark does an excellent job of equating Jesus' encounters with contemporary struggles in life. In *Jesus and the 12 Steps*, you will find the difficult climb out of the hole of addiction. You will read these familiar biblical accounts with a different perspective than you ever have before.

Mike Sandlin
Director – Cape Fear Men
Wilmington, North Carolina

Mark has hit it out of the park with his newest book, *Jesus and the 12 Steps*. He has beautifully put into words the pathway to freedom that is found in the words of Jesus and the limitless truths of the 12-Step principles. I enthusiastically endorse *Jesus and the 12 Steps* as well as Mark's entire There's Still Hope recovery ministry.

Stan Pavlovich
Pastor – Church of the Cross
Bradenton, Florida

Since we met in 2014, I have seen Mark pour himself out for a thirsty, hurting world, from a heart of desperation. In *Jesus and the 12 Steps*, Mark outlines a movement that began 80 years ago, but had its roots in first-century Christianity, and should be embraced by the Church today. This book will help you make the spiritual connection that is vital to recovery.

"Robert L."
Mark's SA Sponsor

Contents

Jesus
AND THE
12 STEPS

THE BIBLICAL RESPONSE TO ADDICTION
IS NOT WHAT YOU THOUGHT

MARK DENISON, D.MIN.

INTRODUCTION

It was a Friday afternoon in Houston, Texas. I had never been to that church before. But there I was—at my first 12-Step meeting.

I arrived early, but sat in my car until 11:59 a.m. I followed a few other men into the large Methodist church, down a hallway, and to the room. I was about to cross a line I never imagined crossing. For a moment, I hesitated. I could still turn and walk away. But I knew I needed to be there. I knew I had a problem. And I knew I couldn't solve this problem myself.

So I did it. Standing on the precipice of an admission I could never take back, I entered the room with the look of a child who mistakenly walked into the wrong bathroom. I felt out of place, out of sorts, and—out of options. I was there because I couldn't get well anywhere else.

Taking a seat in the corner, I was comforted with these instructions: "As a newcomer, you don't need to admit to an addiction. When we introduce ourselves, simply state your first name."

I endured that meeting by telling myself I was surrounded by some really sick people, that my problem didn't rise to their level, and that I could solve my issues with a little more prayer, counseling, and sheer determination. The meeting ended at 1:00 sharp. I was back in my car by 1:05 dull. Confused and frustrated, I felt dehumanized, anxious, and exhausted.

But I had done it. Following the advice of my therapist, I went to a Sex Addicts Anonymous (SAA) meeting. When it was over, I bolted with the burst of an All-American halfback, but I could say I had tried it.

That was in 2001. My wife, Beth, had suspected something was wrong. It became clear that I had a problem. So I reluctantly agreed to attend one meeting. Afterwards, there was little pressure from Beth or my counselor to go back, so I didn't attend another 12-Step meeting.

Until 2013.

After twelve more years of lies, dodges, excuses, and failed attempts to get well, I hit bottom. In November 2013, I was "caught." For the first time, I became desperate to do whatever it took to get sober, even if it meant attending another 12-Step meeting.

So I returned—to the same church on the same day at the same time. But this time, I went in a little early, talked a bit during the meeting, hung out after, and picked up some literature on my way out. It was a small step in the right direction. But that was all it took.

Rich was the facilitator of that meeting. We exchanged cell numbers when it was over. I left feeling something I hadn't felt in years—hope. The next Friday, I returned. I arrived a little earlier and stayed a little longer. And I did one more thing. During that meeting, while we were "checking in," I said nine words for the first time in my life. The emotions of shame and worthlessness flooded over me, reducing me to an emotional mess. But I still got the words out.

"My name is Mark, and I'm a sex addict."

It seems like a lifetime ago. Since that day, I have kept going to meetings. Twice a week, eight times a month, 100 times a year, I have gone back. I've been to SAA, SA (Sexaholics Anonymous), Castimonia, Celebrate Recovery, and AA meetings. When we moved from Texas to Florida in late 2014, I found a 12-Step group before I found a church, a gas station, or the nearest Walmart.

I still attend two meetings a week. I have a sponsor, I sponsor others, and I lead meetings. I have served in several capacities within my groups: facilitator, secretary, literature person, etc. I arrive early and I stay late.

Why do I attend 12-Step meetings? There is only one reason—for me it works. I don't go because my wife wants me to or because I feel pressured to attend. I don't go because I can't find anything else to do 40 minutes from home on Thursday nights and Saturday mornings. I don't go because I enjoy getting up at 6:45 a.m. every Saturday. Between meetings, driving to meetings, and driving home, I spend 250 hours a year on meetings—the equivalent of six 40-hour weeks of work. Why do I do it? I go for just one reason—for me, it works.

Why does it work? I can only speak for myself. These are my thoughts, not taken from any literature or 12-Step materials.

1. **The Steps are biblical.** I'll say more about this later. The purpose of this book is to demonstrate that Jesus' personal ministry validates the 12 Steps. Don't misunderstand me. I'm not putting the 12 Steps on the same level as Scripture—by any means. I believe the Bible is the inspired Word of God, given to us without any mixture of error. But the Steps work because they lead to a path that is very much supported by Scripture.

2. **I need the accountability.** The steps cannot be worked apart from the help of a sponsor. That gives me a level of accountability that I need. It was a lack of accountability that got me into this mess in the first place. The steps provide the accountability that I desperately need.

3. **I need the fellowship.** My 12-Step meetings are the only places I can go where I can talk freely about my "issue." There is no judgment. We are all joined by one common de-

sire to get well. As iron sharpens iron, one member sharpens another.

4. **I learn from others**. Before every meeting I pray the same thing. "May I learn one thing from this meeting that I can use in my own recovery." That prayer has been answered hundreds of times. Sometimes, I learn from the man with 25 years of solid recovery. Other times, I learn from the humility of the man picking up his first 24-hour "desire chip." I learn from the 19-year-old who just found us or the 92-year-old who just found sobriety.

5. **I love the honesty**. A 12-Step room is safe. It is the only place where you can say, "My name is Jeff, and I lost my sobriety this week," and not be judged. Whether you measure your sobriety in days or decades, in a SA or SAA meeting (to name two), you can tell your story without fear of rejection.

That's why I keep going back. I will always be in recovery, so I will always be in meetings. Meetings work and the 12 Steps work. I have heard hundreds of men say, "I worked the Steps and I found sobriety." But I have yet to meet the man who said, "I quit working the Steps to find sobriety."

As we will see in our brief history of the 12 Steps, this is a spiritual program. In fact, that language is ac-

tually in the Steps. Steps 2, 3, 5, 6, 7, 11, and 12 all address this head-on.

Whether this is your first exposure to the 12
Steps, or you have worked the steps several times, it
is our hope that this will bring a fresh perspective to
you. Many believe in Jesus and many believe in the
Steps. My thesis is this: you can believe in Jesus and
the Steps—at the same time.

The Gospel stories that comprise each chapter
were carefully selected from the dozens of real encounters Jesus had with real men and women who
were really struggling with the challenges of life. Other accounts could have been chosen, for every encounter of Jesus with strugglers really fits seamlessly
alongside the Steps. What you will find as you read
each chapter is a God of hope and healing. In fact, our
ministry embraces this message of hope so much that
it defines everything we do. As you will read in every
step and every chapter—**There's Still Hope**.

ACKNOWLEDGMENTS

First, I must acknowledge my Lord and Savior, Jesus Christ. Without Him, there would be no sobriety. Without Him, there could be no recovery. He alone is my "Higher Power," the One whose wisdom inspires me daily. Jesus knows my struggles and fears, because He was tempted in all ways as I am. Jesus was tempted with lust. He knew what it was to maintain custody of His eyes. And one incredible truth I have learned in recovery is this—God is on my side.

Second, I acknowledge my beautiful wife of 36 years. Beth loves me and believes in me. But more than that, she loves Jesus and believes in Him. Through decades of pain, she stood with me. When I pastored (31 years), she sat on the front row every Sunday, smiling, taking notes, and laughing at my jokes when no one else did. Today, she is the premier Partner Recovery Coach in America. She leads women into recovery with her wisdom, insight, training, and mostly, her heart.

Third, I am grateful for every therapist who encouraged me to land in a 12-Step group. Some of them were relentless. They never gave up on me. They knew the value of the Steps, and they wanted me to experience the miracle of grace.

Fourth, I acknowledge two men: Bill W. and Dr. Bob. These brave trailblazers founded Alcoholics Anonymous and wrote the 12 Steps that we still use today. Without them, recovery would be light years behind where it is today.

Fifth, I am grateful for Sexaholics Anonymous. Founded by Roy K in the 1970s, SA is patterned after AA. Unlike other "S" groups, SA offers a clear definition of sobriety that Christ-followers easily embrace. Sober since January 31, 1976, Roy K died from cancer on September 15, 2009. His wisdom, leadership, and 33 years of sexual sobriety provided the framework for recovery that has touched millions of lives around the world—including mine.

Sixth, I acknowledge my sponsor. Robert (not his real name) guided me through the steps with his wisdom, grace, encouragement, and example. For eight years, Robert has continued to "work the steps" himself. I will be forever grateful for his influence in my life.

Seventh, I am thankful for my sponsees. It has been my honor, over the past several years, to help others help themselves. Aside from this ministry (There's Still Hope), I am a sponsor to men who largely know nothing of this ministry. Like my sponsor says, I don't sponsor them for their recovery, but for mine. As of this writing, I am sponsoring 12 men—way too many, but our groups always need sponsors. And nothing blesses me more than watching these guys pick up a chip at the end of a meeting. Each one of them has taught me something about recovery.

Finally, I must acknowledge the immeasurable blessing and influence of Dr. Milton Magness upon my life. Milton and Kathie have become two of our dearest friends and most ardent supporters. Milton is my mentor—a role he did not seek! His investment in my life and ministry is incalculable.

HISTORY OF THE 12 STEPS

The 12 Steps are synonymous with Alcoholics Anonymous. It is impossible to discuss the Steps apart from AA. Since its inception over 80 years ago, AA has grown to 1.8 million members in 87,000 groups meeting in 136 countries. In order to understand the genesis of the Steps, it is helpful to understand the context that became the incubator that gave birth to this international recovery movement.

PROHIBITION

The culture of the early 20th century precipitated the movement that would become Alcoholics Anonymous. The common view of alcoholism was rooted in antiquated thinking as outlined by Dr. Benjamin Rush, who published a landmark work in 1784 titled *Inquiry into the Effects of Ardent Spirits on the Human Mind and Body*. Dr. Rush described alcoholism as a "disease induced by vice."[1] Seeking to help, he started what became known as "sober houses," for those suffering from this disease.

The Temperance Movement of the 1800s gained political clout, which led to complete prohibition of alcohol in 1920. The movement was furthered by the

Women's Christian Temperance Union that began in the late 1800s. All of this was a response to public health issues and domestic violence tied to alcohol abuse. But neither the demeaning of alcoholics nor the ban on the drug diminished the problem.

In post-prohibition America, alcoholism was generally perceived to be a moral failing. The medical community saw alcoholism as incurable and lethal. Heavy drinkers were often relegated to specialized hospitals equipped to confront mental illness. Those without sufficient financial means to access decent medical care were sent to state hospitals, Salvation Army, or less-equipped charitable and religious groups to care for them.

THE OXFORD GROUP

Dr. Franklin Buchman, a Lutheran minister, launched a strong evangelical movement in 1921. Initially known as the First Century Christian Fellowship, the movement became known as the Oxford Group by 1931. Dr. Buchman summarized the group's philosophy with a few simple statements. He believed that sinners could be radically changed if they confessed their sins and need for a Savior. The emphasis on surrender to God would influence the founders of AA greatly. The Oxford Group's American leader was Samuel Moor Shoemaker, Jr., an Episcopalian minister, whose influence on a power greater than man would lay the groundwork for what became the 12 Steps.

A TALE OF TWO MEN

Alcoholics Anonymous was founded on June 10, 1935, by two men: William Griffith Wilson and Dr. Robert Holbrook Smith. Four years later, Wilson wrote what would become known as the AA "Big Book," which still guides the movement 80 years later. Within the book one finds the 12 steps that lead a person to sobriety. Until then, treatment of alcoholism was largely punitive, not redemptive.

BILL WILSON

Known more commonly as Bill W, Wilson's alcoholism had ruined a promising Wall Street career. Wilson also studied law, but was too drunk to walk across the stage to receive his diploma. His drinking ruined his marriage. On at least four separate occasions, his drinking landed him at Towns Hospital, where his doctor, William Silkworth, convinced him that his addiction was a disease, not a moral failure. For the first time, Wilson had hope.

A friend visited Wilson in his New York City apartment and told him that he had experienced a spiritual awakening. This troubled Wilson at first, as he was a nonbeliever. But his drinking was out of control. He knew he needed to do something, but he didn't know what that was.

In a drunken state, Wilson showed up at the Calvary Rescue Mission, where he attended his first Oxford Group meeting. At the altar call, Wilson gave his life to Jesus Christ. But he continued to drink, which landed him in the hospital one last time. Lying in his hospital bed, Wilson cried out to God. "I'll do anything! Anything at all! If there be a God, let him show himself!"

A sense of serenity flooded Wilson's heart, and he was changed. When he was released from the hospital on December 18, 1934, Wilson committed to attending the Oxford meetings regularly. He found sobriety, and soon was on a crusade to bring that sobriety to others.

BOB SMITH

During a business trip in Akron, Ohio, Wilson phoned local ministers in search of alcoholics who wanted help. He was directed to a local Oxford Group that had been trying to help a desperate alcoholic named Dr. Bob Smith.

Dr. Bob began drinking heavily as a student at Dartmouth College. He became a doctor, but his habit nearly ended his practice and marriage early. A friend convinced Smith to meet with Wilson for just 15 minutes. The meeting would last over six hours. Smith quickly embraced the message of Christ and the message of sobriety. He became Wilson's first "convert" to sobriety. He took his last drink on June 10, 1935, which has since been cited as the founding date for Alcoholics Anonymous.[2]

Smith and Wilson soon became partners in their crusade to help others. They began the work of formulating a plan that could be taken to others. Wilson and Smith were committed to the spiritual principles they had discovered in their Oxford meetings. They believed that active alcoholics could not overcome their disease on their own, and that a spiritual conversion was foundational for their recovery.

Two practical elements of their early program soon emerged. The first was that an alcoholic could not find sobriety without the help of another alcoholic. The second principle was that if a man could stay sober for 24 hours, he could stay sober for a lifetime. (This was the foundation for the popular "24-hour chip" still used by all brands of 12-Step groups.)

THE BIG BOOK

Bill W wrote *Alcoholics Anonymous*, known by most as "The Big Book," in 1939. The book includes numerous stories of recovering alcoholics. Five thousand copies sat in a warehouse, as the demand for the book was nonexistent. Then a radio interview with an alcoholic in recovery brought attention to Wilson's work. Popular, affirming articles in *Liberty* magazine and the *Saturday Evening Post* spiked interest, as well.

The AA movement and the "Big Book" began to take off. Further editions and minor changes were published in 1955, 1976, and 2001. While continuing a life of sobriety, Bob Smith helped more than 5,000 alcoholics before his death from colon cancer on November 16, 1950, at the age of 71. Bill Wilson continued to promote his cause until his death from pneumonia on January 24, 1971, at the age of 75.

For more details on the evolution of Alcoholics Anonymous and its founders, it is suggested that you consult Amanda Daniels' work, *A History of the 12 Steps*, and *Why Bill W. Wrote the 12 Steps Twice*, by Susan Cheever.

THE 12 STEPS

After writing chapters three and four of the "Big Book," Wilson changed direction. He felt that a specific plan needed to be included in his work—a plan for sobriety. Referring to principles from the Oxford Group, Wilson developed six basic steps to recovery. In the fall of 1938, he expanded them to twelve steps, breaking each of the original six steps into two parts. The result is what is still known as Chapter Five of the "Big Book." These are the 12 Steps of Alcoholics Anonymous. [The AA terminology for the Steps will be used throughout this book.]

1. We admitted we were powerless over alcohol—that our lives had become unmanageable.
2. Came to believe that a Power greater than ourselves could restore us to sanity.

3. Made a decision to turn our will and our lives over to the care of God as we understood Him.

4. Made a searching and fearless moral inventory of ourselves.

5. Admitted to God, to ourselves, and to another human being the exact nature of our wrongs.

6. Were entirely ready to have God remove all these defects of character.

7. Humbly asked Him to remove our shortcomings.

8. Made a list of all persons we had harmed, and became willing to make amends to them all.

9. Made direct amends to such people wherever possible, except when to do so would injure them or others.

10. Continued to take personal inventory and when we were wrong promptly admitted it.

11. Sought through prayer and meditation to improve our conscious contact with God, as we understood Him, praying only for knowledge of His will for us and the power to carry that out.

12. Having had a spiritual awakening as the result of these Steps, we tried to carry this message to alcoholics, and to practice these principles in all our affairs.

STEP ONE

THE MAN WITH A THOUSAND DEMONS

MARK 5:1-20
"We admitted that we were powerless—that our lives had become unmanageable."

I f ever there was an example of a life that had become unmanageable, this is it. A life more out of control cannot be found—in or out of Scripture. We know little of the man's past, nor are we given more than a glimpse into his future. We encounter this man at his absolute bottom. He had lost all there was to lose—his family, home, business, reputation, and lifestyle. To call him desperate would be to diminish the use of the word desperate.

In stepped Jesus. It was an unexpected encounter, found only on heaven's calendar. Jesus had just finished a long day's ministry on the other side of the lake. He would then set out across stormy seas to see one man—this man. After this "chance" encounter, Jesus would return to the land of Galilee. Sure, there was work to be done on the east side of the lake. There were ten cities in need of the Gospel. But rather than preach to these cities or send his disciples among the masses, Jesus opted for a different strategy. For the cities of Decapolis there was just one hope. That hope rested in the testimony of one man, a man who was known only for his bizarre behavior just a day earlier.

Addict, meet recovery. Crazy, meet sane. Lost, meet saved. Unmanageable, meet manageable. *Legion, meet Jesus.*

JESUS' FIRST STEP ENCOUNTER LEGION

THE PRIORITY OF ONE

"Jesus went across the lake to the region of the Garasenes" (Mark 5:1). The term *Garasenes* literally meant "people of the pilgrimage." These pilgrims were of Syrian descent, and now were mostly Greeks, or Gentiles. Beyond that, we know very little. Certainly, this was not a region of influence, nor did it fit the profile for the ministry of Jesus among the Jews.

Still, Jesus came, if only so briefly. To the crowds, it made no sense—leaving Galilee at nighttime, when storms were common across the Sea of Galilee. But Jesus wasn't playing to the crowds, but to an audience of one. Charles Spurgeon, the well-known preacher of the nineteenth century, stated the obvious: "Knowing a storm was brewing just out of sight, Jesus set his direction, not around the storm, but right into it." Indeed, "a furious squall came up, and the waves broke over the boat, so that it was nearly swamped" (Mark 4:37).

But the Captain of the little ship stayed the course. On the other side of the lake there was no church to greet them, no café to feed them, and no inn to house them. In place of the church, café, and inn there was a cemetery. And in that cemetery awaited one man—a divine appointment.

STEP ONE IN REAL TIME

"A man with an impure spirit came from the tombs to meet him" (Mark 5:2). Here, we find Step 1 lived out in real time. We have a man possessed by countless demons. (Anyone who does not believe in demon possession has never taught a class of two-year-olds.) We have a man beyond the reach of therapy and science. We have a man who meets every definition of insanity. We have a man about to get well. We observe five things about his condition.

First, the man's condition was progressive. Like addiction, it got worse with time. There must have been a time when he could be chained by the strength of others, but that day had passed. We read that they "could not bind him anymore" (Mark 5:3).

Second, all else had failed. Surely, the man's family had tried therapy at the first signs of trouble. Because we know his disease was progressive, a process of intervention must have been exhausted: talks with his family, a visit to a religious leader, counseling, and prayer. Perhaps he had been institutionalized, only to break out. Then he was cast away to the darkness of the cemetery.

Third, he turned to Jesus. Note, Jesus didn't approach him. Rather, the man "came to meet him" (Mark 5:2). Further, "he fell on his knees in front of him" (Mark 5:6). If the man could have managed his condition on his own—or with the help of others—he would have already. He was down to his last straw, and Jesus was that straw.

GRAVEYARD SHIFT

"The man lived in the tombs, and no one could bind him anymore, not even with a chain" (Mark 5:3). The poor man had once been normal; otherwise, we wouldn't read, "no one could bind him *anymore*." There once was a time when he took his place in the house of worship, conducted business with his neighbors, and perhaps carried on a fulfilling family life.

But those days had passed. He had shifted to the graveyard. This graveyard shift was opposite of everything the culture of the day embraced. The law forbid dwelling among the dead or dying. The graveyard shift was void of any interaction with others. It was not safe from the elements. It was the most dire circumstance that life could offer. Cemeteries were set on a hill, to avoid floods. This man's hill became his hell, as in the distance he could see the city where he used to live and the places he used to go. But no more. He would live the rest of his life in his personal prison—the graveyard shift.

OUT OF CONTROL

"No one was strong enough to subdue him" (Mark 5:4). Not the carpenter or craftsman. Not the goldsmith or glass worker, the stonemason or silversmith, the fisherman or farmer. The rancher who had the strength to control the most untamed herd could not tame this one human being.

Notice what Jesus did not do for the man. He did not try to reform him. Jesus didn't give him a set of platitudes or rules. There was no class for which he could sign up, no session to attend, no medicine to swallow. And there was a reason for that. The man had a spiritual condition for which there was only a spiritual solution.

Here's what we know. The man had been in this condition for a long time (Luke 8:27). His condition was progressive (Mark 5:3). He wore no clothes and lived like a wild animal (Luke 8:27). He had supernatural strength and uncontrollable behavior. What had been tried didn't work. Every class, seminar, and pill had fallen short. Why? Because of a misdiagnosis. You don't cast out demons in a psychiatrist's office. (And you don't treat sex addiction apart from the power of God.)

Make no mistake. The 12 Steps are, at their core, a spiritual program. Seven of the steps make direct references to a "Higher Power." The man in our story was out of control. He met all the criteria of the First Step. And that's a good thing, for this set the stage for a pretty incredible outcome.

CORAM DEO

"When he saw Jesus from a distance, he ran and fell on his knees in front of him" (Mark 5:6). In so doing, the demon-possessed man entered into a worship of a God he did not know. Sadly, the same thing happens every Sunday in thousands of churches across the land. It's hard to say what drove him to run to Jesus, exactly. Had he heard about Christ? Was he simply curious? Or just desperate?

We know this. There is something about Jesus that draws others to Him. And there is something about man that creates a longing for something more. Notice, the man didn't just bring his problem to the Great Physician. He brought himself. Early in his faith journey, he was embracing what theologians would come to see as a bedrock for the Christian faith.

Like any pious Augustinian, John Calvin viewed every aspect of life as coram Deo, a Latin phrase meaning "living before the face of God." It was when this crazed maniac bowed before the face of God that healing could begin—and not a moment before.

AN UNLIKELY THEOLOGIAN

"What do you want with me, Jesus, Son of the Most High God?" (Mark 5:7). In Step Three we will encounter the words over which so many addicts stumble: "Made a decision to turn my life and will over to the care of God as I understood God." This is an important point—early recovery does not require complete understanding. Don't miss two key phrases: *the care of God* and *as I understood God*.

Imagine what would have happened if Jesus had told the demoniac, "Figure out this Christianity thing, then come see me." To his credit, the man ran to Jesus. He bowed before him. He even used the right word: *Elion*—"Most High." His mouth ran ahead of his brain. His understanding of Jesus was elementary at best. He hadn't been to a class or studied theology. Still, he knew that the person he was addressing wasn't from this world. He was clearly from on high.

The most unlikely theologian in the Bible, the man came to the right person and he asked the right question: "What do you want with me?" This begs the question. How is it that a man who had never seen Jesus was so intent on meeting him now? How could a man of superhuman strength be willing to bow before a stranger from a foreign land? The answer is encapsulated in a single word. Desperation. He recognized that he was powerless, and that his life had become unmanageable. And this epiphany carried him over the threshold of Step One.

NAME IT AND CLAIM IT

"Jesus asked him, 'What is your name?' 'My name is Legion,' he replied, 'for we are many'" (Mark 5:9). We can finally put a name with a face. His name was Legion. This wasn't his given name, but it was one well-earned.

The word legion was a military term. It identified the size of one's military force. A legion was the largest unit of the Roman army, consisting of 3,000 to 6,000 soldiers. The demons were many—as many as 6,000 if we are to take this literally. Whether 6,000 or just a few hundred, the demons had taken up residency in the man's life.

Herein lies an important point. Before you can treat an illness you must identify it. Let me illustrate.

I'm not good at making things. But there is one thing I make better than almost anyone else on earth. I make kidney stones. I've made at least 70 of them. I'm so good at this that I can do it in my sleep. I can do it on a plane or on a train, while I walk or when I talk. When I'm up and when I'm down, I can make them all around.

No, my physician's name is not Dr. Seuss. But he's good—*real good*. When the next stone hits, I bow in my doctor's presence. I know a kidney stone when

I feel one. Still, when I enter the ER, screaming for something to knock me out, my doctor runs the tests. Why? He has to know what he is treating.

I know a lot of men who cringe at the suggestion that they are an "addict." They may have had dozens of affairs and spent $50,000 on their habit, but they don't want to be called "addict." In order to treat my condition, the doctor has to say "kidney stone." In order for the man in our story to get well, he had to say "Legion." And in order for you to get sober, you have to say it—"I am a sex addict. I am powerless. My life has become unmanageable."

NEGOTIATION

"And he begged Jesus again and again to not send them out of the area" (Mark 5:10). Legion did what we all do. He negotiated with God—"again and again." He wanted healing, but on his own terms. That is our first instinct when we enter recovery. We want the benefits without the cost. We want sobriety without sacrifice and recovery without repentance. After all, our dignity is at stake.

Let's return to my kidney stone illustration. I've had stones treated in many ways. Sometimes, the doctor says to go home and pass the stone. Other times, he suggests lithotripsy. Then there's the "basket procedure" (look it up). But not one time has my urologist said, "I don't know, Mark. *What do you think?*

How would you recommend treating this thing inside of you that is the size of a beach ball?"

There are times in life when negotiation is a good thing—where to eat, what movie to watch, which shirt makes us look fat. But the ER is no place for negotiation. It's a place for total submission. Among the tombstones, Legion had to submit. In the ER, I have to submit. And in your addiction, you have to submit. There's no room for negotiation.

PIGS GONE WILD

"A large herd of pigs was feeding on the nearby hillside. The demons begged Jesus, 'Send us among the pigs; allow us to go into them.' He gave them permission, and the impure spirits came out and went into the pigs. The herd, about two thousand in number, rushed down the steep bank into the lake and were drowned" (Mark 5:11-13).

Recovery comes on God's terms. Some would argue that it doesn't make sense that going to meetings, working the steps, and getting a sponsor would yield lasting sobriety. But just as Naaman had to dip in the muddy waters, the blind man had to take mud in his eye, and the lame man had to pick up his mat—all in order to get well, we too must do things that may not seem to make sense.

We know a few things about pigs in Scripture. We know they were considered "unclean" by the Levitical Law (Leviticus 11:7). We know pigs could not be eaten—or even touched—by faithful Jews. But this was the land of the Garasenes. This was not a Jewish land, but Gentile territory. So Jesus broke all the rules. He featured pigs in this amazing story of restoration.

John Calvin commented on this passage: "It was a magnificent display of the power of Christ, that by his voice not one devil, but a great multitude of devils, were suddenly driven out."[1] The great Healer did what no one else could do. He cast the demons from the man, and the pigs went wild.

THE WORLD'S BEST SERMON

"Those tending the pigs ran off and reported this in the town and countryside, and the people went out to see what had happened. When they came to Jesus, they saw the man who had been possessed by the legion of demons, sitting there, dressed and in his right mind; and they were afraid . . . The man went away and began to tell in the Decapolis how much Jesus had done for him" (Mark 5:14-15, 20).

St. Francis of Assisi is credited with saying, "Preach everywhere, and when necessary, use words." (A better-sourced version has him saying, "It is no use walking anywhere to preach unless our walking is our preaching.")[2] The world's best sermon is one that is watched, not heard. When we get sober, others need to see it (our behaviors) before they hear it (our words). C.S. Lewis wrote, in *Mere Christianity*, "When we Christians behave badly, or fail to behave well, we are making Christianity unbelievable to the outside world."[3]

Before Legion shared his faith, he lived his faith. Before Jesus sent him to share his story in ten different cities, He watched him live his story right where he was. If the propagation of the Gospel was all about words, Jesus would have done more preaching. But He was more into changing lives. Legion's words were authenticated by his changed life. It was only when others saw what God had done *in* him that God could effectively speak *through* him.

UNEXPECTED RESPONSE

"Then the people began to plead with Jesus to leave their region" (Mark 5:17). Say what? Before Jesus appeared on the scene, what they had was a crazy dude, running around naked, cutting himself with rocks, living the life of an unpredictable menace, threatening the lives of all who passed within his reach. Now they had a man "in his right mind."

We see two things here. First, recovery is a scary thing. The people were more afraid of Legion in his right mind than they were of him when he was nuts. From wounded spouses, we hear it all the time. "Take care of your recovery," they tell their husbands. "I don't need to know the details." They say this out of fear. Any power that can heal a man with a thousand demons—or a man with one sex addiction—is scary. So we do what they did two thousand years ago. "Great,

Jesus! You healed the man. Now leave." We want the blessing without the relationship, because the relationship is scary.

Second, we are reminded that most of us prefer a problem we know to a solution we don't. Surely Legion wasn't the only guy within a ten-city region who had problems. Still, they asked Jesus to leave. Of course, they still wanted the benefits of one less crazy man running around naked in the cemetery at night. But they didn't want the rest of the package. Like Legion, they needed Jesus. They just didn't want Him.

ON TO STEP 12

"As Jesus was getting into the boat, the man who had been demon-possessed begged to go with him. Jesus did not let him, but said, 'Go home to your own people and tell them how much the Lord has done for you, and how he has had mercy on you.' So the man went away and began to tell in the Decapolis how much Jesus had done for him. And all the people were amazed" (Mark 5:18-20).

When a football team plays in a rival stadium, the noise and fanfare can be intimidating. The team huddles before every play, as there is comfort in the huddle. In the huddle they are one in purpose. They can lock arms in mutual support. But no one has ever scored a touchdown from the huddle.

Those in recovery need the huddle, but we can't live there. We call these huddles "meetings." We huddle in rooms across the globe every hour of every day. Some wear the letters "SA" (Sexaholics Anonymous) across their jersey. Others play for SAA (Sex Addicts Anonymous) or CR (Celebrate Recovery). Each group huddles up. And these huddles are critical; otherwise, the players wouldn't know how to run the right route.

Legion wanted to join the holy huddle of Jesus and the twelve. He literally begged to stay with his new friends, to learn from them, travel with them, and grow with them. But Jesus said, "No."

By sending Legion back to his homeland of Decapolis (ten cities), a largely Gentile area, Jesus was saying, "Skip to the Twelfth Step. Tell others what I have done for you." Jesus had a plan for Decapolis. But that plan didn't include his preaching or the work of the twelve disciples. Jesus' plan was to use one changed life.

To the untrained eye, this would not appear to be an impactful move on Jesus' part. But only heaven will tell us the results of this unexpected move. You see, these ten cities formed an alliance for protection and increased trade opportunities. Such was the greatness of these cities that the remains of one of them— Scythopolis—can be seen to this day.

Jesus knew there were people Legion could reach that Peter and John could not. The same is true for you. God has uniquely gifted you and placed you so that you can make a difference—if you skip to the Twelfth Step: "Having had a spiritual awakening . . . we tried to carry this message to addicts and to practice these principles in all our affairs."

When the founders of Alcoholics Anonymous (Bill Wilson and Bob Smith) developed the 12 Steps, it was their intent that addicts would "work the steps" in one month. While this is not usually wise, we need to jump ahead to Step Twelve from the first day. There are always those in our lives to whom we can carry the message of hope.

No one cares what is going on in your meetings, church services, or holy huddles. They do care about what is going on in your life. Do what Legion did. When you are ready to admit that your life is out of control, when you can label your problem for what it is, and when you accept that your life is unmanageable, you are ready to experience freedom. And then you will want to carry this message to as many as you possibly can.

STEP TWO

THE MAN LOWERED THROUGH THE ROOF

LUKE 5:17-26

"We came to believe that a Power greater than ourselves could restore us to sanity"

Fresh off the selection of his 12 disciples and the healing of a leper, Jesus was confronted by a man who was the epitome of the Second Step. While we will camp out in Luke 5, this story is also told by two other writers—Matthew and Mark, who fill in some additional data points. For example, Mark tells us the setting for this story—the city of Capernaum (Mark 2:1). Matthew reminds us that this was Jesus' "home town" (Matthew 9:1).

The setting is not immaterial. Capernaum was the ideal place for this miracle for several reasons. First, Jesus was well known in his hometown and he had just performed several miracles. This would result in a full house, which explained the difficulty the paralytic had in getting close to Jesus. Second, Capernaum was a city of influence. As a banking center and place of trade, when something newsworthy took place in Capernaum, it became widely known. Therefore, the story before us would be told far and wide within days. Third, the area was home to religious leaders and teachers of the Law. What Jesus did was intentional; so was the place He did it. He welcomed the skepticism that would fill the house that day.

What ensued would be one of the most famous of Jesus' 40 miracles, recorded in three Gospels and repeated for thousands of years. As the story unfolds, we find Jesus teaching the multitudes in a crowded house, when a paralytic's friends (Mark 2:3 says there were four of them) carry him to that house in order to meet the great healer. Unable to enter through the door, due to the large crowd, they got creative. They ascended to the roof, carrying their buddy with them, then dug a hole in the roof and lowered their friend to Jesus. Christ then healed the man—first of his sin, then of his paralysis. At Jesus' command, the man picked up his mat and walked home, praising God.

Let's dig deeper. This amazing account features six unique individuals/groups. We will tell the story from each of their vantage points. Then we will make the case that this amazing story is a test case for Step Two.

JESUS' SECOND STEP ENCOUNTER
SIX WITNESSES

JESUS

Make no mistake—Jesus is the central figure in this story. While the paralytic would not have been healed apart from working the Second Step, his seminal moment was only made possible by the orchestration of circumstances created by the one he had yet to meet. We see three things about Jesus.

First, Jesus was *intentional*. It was no coincidence that Jesus was where He was when He was there. He picked that city—Capernaum, the paralytic's hometown. He chose *that day*—when the crowds were most curious on the heels of the leper's healing. He chose *that crowd*—where the religious leaders would be present. He chose *that location*—where the paralytic and his friends could come. And he chose *that house*—knowing it would be so small that they would have to make a scene in order to get the sick man to Him.

Second, Jesus was *approachable*. On the road to raise Jairus' daughter, he paused for the woman who was sick. Entering Jericho, He paused to meet Zaccheaus. Walking at night, He paused to hear Nicodemus. And on this day, He chose a living room as His sanctuary, and His neighbors as His congregation. Those who wanted to hear Him were allowed to crowd in so tight that He had to stand. (Teachers generally remained seated.) And then, when the paralytic had no way to get to Him, He welcomed the intrusion through the roof, in the middle of a teaching moment.

Third, Jesus was *influential*. He understood leadership before John Maxwell wrote his first book. Jesus understood that while you impress from a distance, you influence up close. Which miracle do you think the attendees in the house that day told their grandchildren about 50 years later—the feeding of the 5,000, the changing of the water into wine, the raising of Lazarus, or the miracle they saw right in front of their own eyes, where they could literally touch the man who was healed? Jesus had in His audience that day some of the most respected religious scholars of the time. But on this occasion, they became the students, and with this healing, class was dismissed.

THE HOME OWNER

When I was new in my faith, I used to regret that there wasn't much I could do to serve God. I was 14, had to hitch a ride to church—or walk—and had little support from others. Still, I wanted to serve. Then my pastor said one Sunday: "God doesn't need your ability as much as he wants your availability."

The homeowner in our story was available. One of the most profound miracles in Scripture occurred in his house, but we know very little about him. If this had been a movie, he would have barely made the list of credits, somewhere between "gaffer" and "key grip."

But we know this—when Jesus needed a stage for an event that would never be forgotten, he was available.

What do we know about this man? He must have had a relationship with Jesus. (Jesus wouldn't have invaded the home of a stranger.) He was not the kind of man to sue someone for making a hole in his roof. He was happy to serve in the background. He was a simple man. But mostly, he was just available. And that is exactly the kind of man Jesus still uses today.

THE RELIGIOUS LEADERS

"As he was teaching, there were Pharisees and teachers of the law sitting by" (Mark 2:1). Luke confirms that these religious leaders had traveled as far as 80 miles to be there (the distance from Jerusalem to Capernaum). Yet, of all who were in the house that day, it was the men who had traveled the greatest distance who remained the furthest from Jesus. But Jesus was not about to run them off. Spurgeon commented on this passage: "We are glad to have these people 'sitting by' rather than not coming at all. Being in the way, the Lord may meet with them. If you go where shots are flying you may be wounded one of these days. Better to come and hear the gospel from a low motive than not to come at all."[1]

We know three things about these "Pharisees and teachers of the law." First, they had *presence without passion*. They were closer to Jesus than anyone, sitting by Him (Mark 2:1). Throughout His entire discourse, they could have reached out and touched the master teacher. They were that close. But when the miracle came, their joy went. While everyone else responded with their hearts, the Pharisees responded with their minds.

Second, the Pharisees had *reason without relationship*. When the paralytic was gloriously healed, they retreated to their theological corners. "The Pharisees and the teachers of the law began to reason" (Luke 5:21). Another translation says they "began thinking to themselves." While the rest of the crowd rejoiced, they criticized. Jesus had the audacity to step beyond their theological lines. This could not stand.

Third, they demonstrated *interest without involvement*. "Pharisees" meant "separated ones." They were to be different. But while others stood, they sat. While others carried their friend to Jesus, they watched with critical eyes. They were zealous and devoted. But their religion left them in the stands, playing the part of the critic. In the process, they missed out on the blessings of God.

THE CROWD

What I'd give to have been there that day! We know almost nothing about the general crowd that filled the room. Though they probably made up 90 percent of the number present, only two verses even mention them. We only know what we read: "When they could not find a way to do this because of the crowd, they went up on the roof and lowered him on his mat through the tiles into the middle of the crowd, right in front of Jesus" (Luke 5:19). Then, after the healing, we read, "Everyone was amazed and gave praise to God. They were filled with awe and said, 'We have seen remarkable things today'" (Luke 5:26). But in these brief references, we deduce three things.

They were curious enough to show up. Surely, there were a lot of other places the crowd could have been that day. They could have reclined at home, shopped at the market, or fished by the lake. They could have conducted business, spent time with family, or attended a public event. But there was something deep in each of their hearts that created a sense of curiosity. They wondered what would happen that day. They were curious enough to show up.

They were receptive enough to listen up. When Jesus spoke, they listened. Even when they heard the roof caving in overhead, none of them left. They knew the place where they stood was somehow holy ground. And they knew that Jesus was not like any other rabbi they had ever heard. They didn't understand everything yet. But they were receptive, so they listened up.

They were excited enough to stand up. They probably knew the paralytic. Many of them had probably donated money to his 'Go Fund Me' account. They had taken him to doctors, cared for his family, and prayed for his healing; thus, when their buddy was suddenly made well, his friends stood and cheered.

THE PARALYTIC

We know at least three things about the paralytic. The most obvious is that he had *friends*. Four men thought enough of him to take a day's vacation, go to his house, create some cords, tie them to his bed, bring some roof removal tools, then carry him down the street. Further, they were willing to risk their own reputation, pay for a new roof, and interrupt Jesus— all in an attempt to give their friend one last shot at walking.

Second, we know the man had *faith*. Though we never hear him speak, we know what he is thinking—"This just might work!" Some time between the guys tying the knot on the cords and picking up his bed, he could have called it off. Somewhere on the road to the neighbor's house, he could have said, "No thanks." Somehow on the lift to the roof, he could have changed his mind. But he didn't. Why? Because he had faith. Yes, Jesus commended the faith of his friends, but surely the man wasn't carried against his will. The man had faith.

Third, the man had *family*. No, we don't read about a mom, a dad, a wife, or any kids. But Jesus told him to go home (Luke 5:25). One thing seems certain. As a paralytic he could not have lived by himself. He either lived in a special home for fellow paralytics or he lived with a caring family at home. Jesus said he had a home.

Consider the difference a few minutes make. The paralytic left home paralyzed, "unable to move his body" (Luke 5:18); he came back walking. He left hopeful of what might be; he came back praising God for what was. And he left home as a sinner, but returned as a saint. Note the progression.

The man was paralyzed—completely. Had he been able to walk even a little bit, he would not have come on a stretcher. He hit bottom; he was desperate. It was thought that such ailments were the result of sinful living. While we can't be sure, it is evident that his disease (like addiction) was progressive. We make this assumption based on Jesus' final words to him: "I tell you, get up, take your mat and go home" (Luke 5:24). If the man had never walked before, he wouldn't know how to walk now. His disease was likely progressive.

But before Jesus healed him, He healed him—spiritually. The man's desire was obvious; he wanted to walk again. But Jesus did the greater miracle first. "When Jesus saw their faith, he said, 'Friend, your sins are forgiven'" (Luke 5:20). Then, after a word with the Pharisees, the same Jesus who brought life to the man's soul now brought life to his legs. "I tell you, get up, take up your mat and go home" (Luke 5:24). In a moment, a crippled sinner became a walking saint.

THE FOUR FRIENDS

The 1972 Miami Dolphins did what no team had ever done in the first 52 years of the National Football League. And it has not been done since. They went undefeated, while winning the Super Bowl. Coach Don Shula identified four things that he said made his team special: (a) each player loved every other player, (b) they had a willingness to do whatever it took, (c) they had a plan, and (d) they were committed to follow through with their plan. The same was true for the four men who led their team to victory, as recorded in Matthew 9, Mark 2, and Luke 5.

First, they loved their friend. While we don't know the genesis of the relationship, these four friends demonstrated an undeniable affection for their friend. This was probably not the first time they had carried his mat. In years past, they had likely carried him to the doctor, market, and place of worship. They wouldn't have done what they did this day had they not loved their paralyzed friend.

Second, the men were willing to do whatever was necessary for their friend to find healing. This included the following risks: personal reputation, legal jeopardy, replacing the roof, financial expenditures, whatever it took. In fact, going in, they didn't know what it would take, exactly. But whatever that was, they were up for the task.

Third, the men had a plan. They had clearly thought this thing out. The plan involved several steps:

(a) ascertain Jesus' schedule, (b) convince the paralytic, (c) bring the cords and tools to his home, (d) tie the cords to his bed, (e) carry the bed down the street, (f) lift the bed to the roof, (g) dig out a hole in the roof, then (h) lower the bed. Every step was a critical part of the plan.

Fourth, the friends were committed to follow-through. They actually went to the man's house. They tied the cords or ropes to his bed. (Mark uses the Latin term *grabatus*, meaning "rude pallet.") Then they actually picked up the bed and marched down the street. When they were unable to bring their friend through the door, they were ready. Up to the rooftop they went. Then, after digging a hole, while the crowd looked up, the paralytic came down.

STEP TWO IN ACTION

"We came to believe that a Power greater than ourselves could restore us to sanity" (Step Two). This Step does not come easily. Notice, *we came to believe.* We did not believe innately or immediately. Faith is a process, not just an event. Next, we recognize a *Power greater than ourselves.* Healing cannot come apart from that power. This power *could restore us.* It's not automatic. There's an oft-repeated line from addiction literature: "Without God I can't; without me, God won't." Yes, God *could* restore us, but only with our willing participation. What does he restore us to? To *sanity.* Does that sound strong—the idea that sex addicts have lost their sanity? If you say yes, you haven't attended a SA meeting.

In what ways does the story of the paralytic epitomize Step Two? As we have already seen, both the man and his friends were committed to this truth—only a Power greater than their own could bring about the healing for which the paralytic had longed. So convinced were they that Jesus had that power that inaction was no longer an option. Planning their next move around Jesus' itinerary was off the table. They had to act now. For them, Jesus was not a *good* option; He was their *only* option. Real faith calls for real action. Consider the following evidence.

THEY COULDN'T WAIT

We don't know how long the meeting in the house had been going. Nor do we know if the four friends waited outside for a time, in hopes that Jesus would come out. But there is no reason to believe the gathering inside would have lasted more than a couple of hours. They could have waited until the Master exited the house. That would have saved a lot of trouble. After all, their buddy had been crippled for years. What difference would a couple more hours make? But they were desperate. Their friend's healing must not wait another minute.

THEY KEPT COMING

I can hear the conversation, as they carried the man several blocks down the road. "Where are you going with Matt?" (That seems an appropriate name for the paralytic.) "We are taking him to see Jesus," they replied. "Don't you know the house is already full? You'll never get inside!" "We are prepared for that," they said, while displaying their tools. The neighbors persisted, "So you're saying that you are going to climb up on the roof, tear a hole in that roof, then lower Matt to the ground?" "Yes, that's what we're saying." And they continued on their journey, when most would have reconsidered and turned back.

THEY DIDN'T KNOCK ON THE DOOR

It became immediately clear that the house was full. They must have suspected that, or they wouldn't have brought their roof removal kit with them. Still, the natural thing to do would have been to knock on the door. "Can Jesus come out for a second?" they might have asked. But they didn't want to risk being told to leave, so they quickly devised a better plan. What would have been anyone else's Plan B was actually their Plan A.

MATT WAS ALL IN

The first few thousand times I read this story, it was like the paralytic was an extra in the play. The story was all about four crazy guys who were just gutsy enough to carve up another man's roof in order to lower their friend to Jesus. Matt was merely a willing accomplice. But let's be clear. The man couldn't move

(Luke 5:18). But none of the biographers (Matthew, Mark, or Luke) ever indicated he could not speak. At any point from the moment the plan was hatched, Matt could have backed out. He could have asked for a house call from Jesus. But Matt was desperate, so he went all in.

THEY SCALED THE ROOF

It's true, this wasn't the feat it would be today. Most houses in this area had stairs in the back. The roof was a place where homeowners often went—to sit, pray, or visit with others. In fact, God did some of His best work on roofs. It was on a roof that Rahab concealed the spies (Joshua 2:6). It was on a roof that Samuel talked with King Saul (1 Samuel 9:25). It was on a roof that David talked with God (2 Samuel 11:2). And it was on a roof that Peter went to pray (Acts 10:9). But these guys carried someone with them to the roof. Not an easy task, they did so because they knew that immediately under that roof was a power greater than themselves that could restore Matt completely.

THEY BROKE THE LAW

In the third century, Rabbi Simlai mentioned in a sermon that the Talmud (Jewish law) included 613 commandments.[2] "Thou shalt not carve up thy neighbor's roof" is not among them. But each community had its own laws. Ripping a hole in a neighbor's roof crossed any line of legal behavior. By carving up the roof, these four men put themselves in legal jeopardy. Worse, there were several dozen eyewitnesses to their crime. But again, it didn't matter. If they would have to spend a few days in jail, it would be worth it, as long as they got their friend to Jesus.

THEY HAD TO BUY A NEW ROOF

Someone would have to pay for a new roof. That someone was clearly Matt's four friends. And they knew it before they removed the first tile or cut the first slice. But that was okay with them, because the cost of a new roof would be a small price to pay for a man's salvation and healing. They were willing to try anything, do anything, and pay anything it took to give their friend an audience of one.

THEY IGNORED THE RELIOUS LEADERS

Let's go back to the beginning of our story. "One day Jesus was teaching, and Pharisees and teachers of the law were sitting there" (Luke 5:17). When the crowd looked up, Matt came down. And as his buddies peered through the hole in the roof, they recognized their friends and neighbors—and the religious scholars of the day. Every one of them knew the Old Testament. They had kept the commandments. They were seminarians, intellects, and serious followers of the law. Surely, among this group of esteemed academics there was much wisdom. But what did the men do? "Lay him before Jesus" (Luke 5:18). Notice, they didn't take him to "the Pharisees," "the teachers of the law," or even "Jesus and the Pharisees/teachers of the law." They ignored the religious leaders, some of whom they may have known personally. Why? Because they were in search of a "power greater than themselves," and they recognized the source of that power.

STEP THREE

THE PRODIGAL SON

LUKE 15:11-32

"We made a decision to turn our will and our lives over to the care of God as we understood Him."

Though raised by two godly parents, William chose the life of a rebel. When he was just 13, his mom and dad sent him away to Stony Brook, a boarding school in New York. In high school, he was suspended for fighting. William broke the curfew rules repeatedly as he indulged in alcohol. Once out of high school, his parents sent him away to a Christian university, which quickly expelled him for his unruly behavior. Eventually, in his 20s, William's life was transformed while on a trip to the holy land. The prodigal returned to the faith of his childhood. You may know him by his full name: William Franklin Graham.

Mikhail Kalashnikov invented the AK-47 in his attempt to protect his Soviet homeland from the Germans in WWII. He was a military general, inventor, engineer, writer, and arms designer. And Mikhail was something else—a committed atheist. He was born in 1919, was a hero in the war, and was a fervent crusader for his faith—or lack of faith—for 70 years. Then, in 1989, Mikhail encountered a leader of the Russian Orthodox Church. He had met his match, a follower of Christ, who extended a grace that Mikhail had never witnessed. He had to know more. Soon, he decided to turn his will and life over to the care of God as he understood God. What resulted was not only a changed life, but a crusade to tell others about Christ, which only ended with Mikhail's death at the age of 93.

We can identify with a prodigal son (or daughter) because we've been one. Such was the life of Franklin Graham. And Mikhail Kalashnikov. And you.

We have before us today perhaps the most famous illustration in the Bible. It is what William Barclay referred to as "the greatest short story in the world."[1] It is what we best know as the parable of the prodigal son.

JESUS' THIRD STEP ENCOUNTER THE SETTING

Parables are illustrations, and Jesus told a lot of them. In fact, the Bible says Jesus did not teach without using parables (Mark 4:34). Luke 15 is no exception. In these verses, we find three profound stories. To best understand them, we must recognize the setting for the telling of these stories—the background, context, and theology. We will get to Step Three shortly, but first, let's unpack the broader context of the most famous of all Jesus' stories.

THREE STORIES

Jesus tells the stories of a (a) lost sheep, (b) lost coin, and (c) lost son. In the story of the lost sheep, the shepherd left 99 behind in his search for the one that was lost (Luke 15:4-7). In the story of the lost coin, the woman with ten silver coins did a "careful search" for the one that was lost (Luke 15:8-10). And in the parable of the lost son, the father anxiously waited for his younger son's return, while his other son had never left home (Luke 15:11-32).

Notice the math: from 1/100 to 1/10 to 1/2. There is an interesting nuance. While the shepherd and the woman were diligent in their search, the father remained back at the ranch. He didn't chase after the lost son. We'll see more on that later.

THE AUDIENCE

The passage begins, "Now the tax collectors and sinners were all gathering around to hear Jesus. But the Pharisees and the teachers of the law muttered, 'This man welcomes sinners and eats with them'" (Luke 15:1-2). Clearly, Jesus' audience was the Pharisees. In response to the muttering religious crowd, he told these parables. And this is important as we unpack the central message of the prodigal son. I suggest the main character was not the son who left home, but the one who stayed. Why? Because he represented the Pharisees. He was them—self-righteous and full of pride. The son who stayed home thought he actually deserved the blessing of his father.

THE MAIN CHARACTERS

First, we have the benevolent father. He was a good man, by all appearances. And he loved his sons. Surely, he knew the trouble his younger son would get into if he granted his wish for an early inheritance. But like the heavenly Father, he allowed his son to exercise free will. According to Jewish law, the father was not free to leave his property however he wanted. The elder son would receive two-thirds of the estate, with the rest going to the younger brother (Deuteronomy 21:17).

Second, we have the younger brother. His story consumes the most space (Deut. 15:11-24). He asked his father for his inheritance, then wasted it in a "far country." Eventually, after he came to his senses, he came to his father. He returned, happy to live out his life as a hired servant; instead, he was reinstated into the family.

Third, we see the older brother (Deut. 15:25-32). Pompous, self-righteous, and self-absorbed, he was the only one who didn't celebrate his brother's return. In his mind, his brother had not suffered enough for his mistakes, and he himself had not been recognized enough. He felt diminished by his brother's return. There are really two prodigals in this story—the one who left and the one who stayed home. But for our purposes of discussing Step Three, we will limit the rest of our study to the younger brother.

ACT I

IN SEARCH OF THE BOTTOM
LUKE 15:11-16

The first act of the prodigal's story finds him running away from home and getting into all kinds of trouble. Clearly, his life had become unmanageable, and he was powerless to do anything about it. St. Augustine reduced the man's story to simple terms: "It is not reason which turns a young man from God; it is the flesh."[2] Let's break down the man's search for his true bottom, verse by verse.

VERSE 12

"The younger one said to his father, 'Father, give me my share of the estate.' So he divided his property between them." Notice, the father did not try to protect his son from his true bottom. He had provided all he could. The son was now a grown man, able to make his own decisions. Similarly, God allows his sons and daughters to plunge into the depths of addiction. Why? Because God allows what he hates in order to accomplish what he loves.

VERSE 13

"Not long after that, the younger son got together all he had, set off for a distant country, and he squandered his wealth in wild living." That's what addiction does. It takes you to a "distant country" unlike anything you've ever known. In seeking your *high* you find an unbearable *low*. You can chase after the "distant country," but know it will cost you. From there, you will lose all contact with family, friends, and all who love you most.

The man left home; then he fell into a hole "not long after that." Once you leave the warmth of your spiritual relationship, what follows doesn't take long. The trip toward the far country of unmanageability is a short one. And then you discover that you can ruin in a few minutes what took a lifetime to build.

He spent his fortune on "wild living." The Greek word is *asotos*, meaning "without abandon." The son was out of control. His addiction to the wild life cost him more than he wanted to pay and it kept him longer than he wanted to stay.

VERSE 14

"After he had spent everything, there was a famine in that whole country, and he began to be in need." Before he could come back, he had to hit bottom. Notice, he didn't save even a little money for the trip home. He didn't save anything for food or lodging. He "spent everything." That's insanity. That's addiction—doing the same behavior over and over, despite negative consequences. And then a famine spread throughout the land. The man's circumstances were beyond anything he could control.

VERSE 15

"So he went and hired himself out to a citizen of that country, who sent him to his fields to feed pigs." Things went from worse to worst. The original text literally reads, "He glued himself to a citizen of that country." This is significant. Being a "far country," the citizens there were not Jewish. They did not recognize the prodigal's God. Don't miss the process: he (a) saw them, (b) joined them, and (c) became them. It was against religious law for a Jew to even touch a pig; now he finds himself feeding pigs. Surely he had hit bottom, right? Now he was ready to move to **Step 3**, right? Not yet. Rarely does a man get help until his problem has cost him something. And for the prodigal son, his mistakes had not yet cost him enough.

VERSE 16

"He longed to fill his stomach with the pods that the pigs were eating, but no one gave him anything." It is amazing how much *bad* can look *good* when you hit bottom. Vance Havner mused, "Had this been the social gospel, someone would have given the man a sandwich and bag of chips, and he would have never returned home."[3] But the inconvenient truth is that we have to find our bottom before we find ourselves.

REVIEW

Let's review. The prodigal was greedy. ("I want my inheritance.") The prodigal was impatient. ("I want it now.") The prodigal was disrespectful. ("I'm not going to wait for dad to die.") The prodigal left his covenant community. ("I will join the pagan crowd.") The prodigal was reckless. ("I will waste my money on wild living.") The prodigal became a slave to his own intentions. ("I will hire myself out.") The prodigal was unclean. ("I'll feed pigs if I have to.")

And now, the prodigal was ready . . .

ACT II
THE ROAD BACK
LUKE 15:17-24

Augustine had it right. He told God, "You never depart from us, but yet, only with difficulties do we return to you."[4] The prodigal son had great difficulties; only then was he ready to work Step 3. The man had hit bottom. He was at a crossroads. It was decision time. Tony Robbins said, "It is in your moments of decision that your destiny is shaped."[5] And John Maxwell wrote, "Life is a matter of choices, and every choice you make makes you."[6] The prodigal had made a series of bad choices. Now it was time for one good decision—a decision that would change everything.

VERSE 17

"When he came to his senses, he said, 'How many of my father's hired servants have food to spare, and here I am starving to death!'" Only when he came to his senses was he ready to come to his father. For every addict, there must be that "aha" moment when the light comes on. Notice what went through the man's mind. He longed to be one of "his father's hired servants." That's important. As a land-owner, his father had two tiers of servants. The top tier consisted of laborers who had security. They were treated like family. But the second-tier workers (hired servants) could be dismissed without notice. So desperate was the younger son that he was willing to go back home, even if for a moment. There would be no guarantees. But he had to try.

VERSE 18

"I will set out and go back to my father and say to him, 'Father, I have sinned against heaven and against you.'" That is owning it. That is working the steps. The man is acknowledging that his "bottom" was on him completely. As I have said many times, I don't apologize for my addiction, but I do apologize for not doing anything about it sooner. If you are living in your addiction today, you must own it. No matter how much trauma and abuse you have experienced, the blame game must stop. Until you can say "I have sinned" and put a period after it (not a comma), you won't be ready to get well.

VERSE 19

"I am no longer worthy to be called your son; make me like one of your hired servants." Now it gets really interesting. Count the number of words in the son's prepared speech. You should get 27. Remember that number; it will matter in a bit.

VERSE 20

"So he got up and went to his father. But while he was still a long way off, his father saw him and was filled with compassion for him; he ran to his son, threw his arms around him, and kissed him." Notice that the father was looking in the direction of the far country, but he didn't chase after his son. He was ready to reconcile with his son anytime his son was ready. The father waited to be wanted. But when he could see his son in the distance, he couldn't help himself. He ran to his son, embraced him, and then the original text says he "kissed him over and over." Such a move on the part of the wanderer was worthy of celebration.

VERSE 21

"The son said to him, 'Father, I have sinned against heaven and against you. I am no longer worthy to be called your son.'" Remember our number from verse 19? The son's prepared speech consisted of 27 words. Now was his chance to deliver that speech. And he did—verbatim. That's how we know the speech was memorized. He didn't miss a word. But count the words of his actual speech (compared to the 27 words of his prepared speech). He came up short—just 19 words. He never got to "Make me like one of your hired servants." His father would have none of it. He cut him off. That is a picture of prayer. God hears our hearts before the words cross our lips. The son had no right to ask to be received back into the family, but his father did for him what he could not do for himself.

VERSE 22

"But the father said to his servants, 'Quick! Bring the best robe and put it on him. Put a ring on his finger and sandals on his feet.'" Here's the rich significance of what the father did. The robe represented honor. The ring signified authority. And the sandals were to be worn only by immediate family. The prodigal had worked his third step, and it paid dividends. When we turn our wills and our lives over to the care of God, we will never be disappointed.

VERSE 23

"Bring the fatted calf and kill it. Let's have a feast and celebrate." Notice what the father said. "Bring the fatted calf—the one set apart for the most special of celebrations." It was time for a party like this ranch had never seen.

VERSE 24

"He said, 'For this son of mine was dead and is alive again; he was lost and is found.' So they began to celebrate." Notice, the prodigal never quit being his father's son. The relationship was still intact, but not the blessings. The son of a king was living like the son of a pauper. Sin does that to us. Addiction does that. But when the son made a decision to turn his will and life over to the care of his father, that all changed. A life that had become completely unmanageable was now filled with hope. And it felt really, really good.

THE THIRD STEP

In the movie *The Number 23*, Jim Carrey's character said, "There's no such thing as destiny. There are only choices."[7] Life is full of choices. A recent study conducted at Columbia University found that we make 70 "significant" decisions every day. Indeed, the prodigal son had become the sum total of a series of bad decisions. He had no one to blame but himself. He suffered from what C.S. Lewis called the "invincible ignorance of his intellect."

What seemed to make sense to the prodigal son seems to make sense to many of us, as well. His life had become unmanageable, and it didn't take long.

But his return was one step away—the Third Step. Once he made the decision to turn his life over to his father—and trust him to make him a slave, servant, or treasured son—the celebration could begin.

Theologian Henri Nouwen wrote a helpful book— *The Return of the Prodigal Son: A Story of Homecoming.* Nouwen brilliantly lays it out for us . . .

Addiction might be the best word to explain the lostness that so deeply permeates society. Our *addictions* make us cling to what the world proclaims as the keys to self-fulfillment: accumulation of wealth and power; attainment of status and admiration; lavish consumption of food and drink; and sexual gratification without distinguishing between lust and love. These *addictions* create expectations that cannot but fail to satisfy our deepest needs. As long as we live within the world's delusions, our addictions condemn us to futile quests in 'the distant country,' leaving us to face an endless series of disillusionments while our sense of self remains unfulfilled. In these days of increasing *addictions*, we have wandered far away from our Father's home. The *addicted* life can aptly be designated a life lived in a "distant country." It is from there that our cry for deliverance rises up.[8]

In Step One, we acknowledge that our lives had become unmanageable and that we are powerless to make a course correction on our own. In Step Two, we acknowledge that there is a God who can save us. And in Step Three, we make a decision—the most important decision of all.

HOW IT WORKS

Until you have visited the "distant country," you will never fully appreciate life back on the Father's ranch. G.K. Chesterton said it well: "It was his home now. But it could not be his home until he had gone from it and returned to it. Now he was the Prodigal Son."⁹

Anyone who doubts the biblical support for the 12 Steps has not read this story. The prodigal son (really both of them) stands as a bright light for Step 3. His life had become a wreck until he made one right decision. In contrast, we see the rich young ruler (Mark 10:17-22) who made one wrong decision.

One of my favorite movies is *Castaway*, starring Tom Hanks. He plays the role of Chuck Noland, an obsessively punctual FedEx executive. On assignment to Malaysia, his plane crashes over the Pacific Ocean during a storm. The only survivor, Chuck washes ashore on a deserted island, where he is stranded for years. His only companion is "Wilson," his volleyball. Ready to risk everything in an effort to get off the island, Chuck made a decision. [I will clean up his language.] "I would rather take my chance out there on the ocean than to stay and die on this %?#@!& island, spending the rest of my #$^#%* life talking to a @*#!$<% volleyball!"

Step Three is your only way off the island. It is the only way to break free of the isolation and the pain. You can try other ways, but you will never get far off the island.

The story of the prodigal son is the story of Step Three. The man had it all, then he traded it all in for a shot at the far country. He didn't know what was out there for him, but he just had to have a look. This obsession to find this "distant country" led him to unimaginable depths of sorrow, loss, and pain.

Every addict understands this pain. But they must not miss the key to the whole story—the eight missing words. When the prodigal plotted his return, he planned the perfect speech. But the Father isn't into speeches. The prodigal's father could recognize his son—and Step Three—a mile away. The decision had been made. The son began his walk home all alone. But it didn't end that way.

Just as the prodigal's father met him on the road back, your Father waits for you. Step Three isn't about the destination as much as the direction. When the son started back in the right direction, the father made sure he'd reach his destination. That promise can be yours—if you decide to turn your will and life over to the care of God.

STEP FOUR

THE SAMARITAN WOMAN

JOHN 4:4-26

"We made a searching and fearless moral inventory of ourselves."

It's the Step that sticks. More 12-steppers get stuck on Step Four than anywhere else in their recovery. Why? This is the Step that calls for an accounting of one's fears, resentments, and character defects—referred to as "instincts gone astray" in AA jargon. The Fourth Step requires hard work, painful introspection, and unyielding honesty. It is to recovery what a colonoscopy is to any man who has had the misfortune of turning 40.

I heard about a boy who used a pay phone (it was a few years ago) to make a call. A stranger stood by, waiting to use the phone when the boy had finished his call. He overheard the boy's conversation.

The boy called a woman, offering his services to mow her yard. When the lady said she already had a boy who mowed her yard, the boy persisted, offering to do it for half of whatever she was paying now. The lady kindly rejected his offer, as she said the boy currently mowing her grass was too good to replace, even at half price.

When the boy hung up the phone, the stranger next to him offered him a job. "I couldn't help but hear your conversation with that woman. I can use boys like you. Come work for me."

"I can't," said the boy. "I already have a job. I mow that lady's yard. I was just calling to see if I'm doing a good job."

Step Four is recovery's way of telling you if you're doing a good job.

We see a picture of the Fourth Step in John 4. Jesus had an unexpected encounter with an unsuspecting woman. What followed was a remarkable example of Step Four.

JESUS' FOURTH STEP ENCOUNTER
AN AMAZING STORY

It's almost as if Jesus said, "Okay, everyone, watch this—the Fourth Step in real time." The story before us could be told on so many dimensions. Our task is not to find truths that apply to Step Four, but to decide which of these truths to leave out. The story of the Samaritan woman provides a light into the soul of every addict and a hope that has eluded so many. It is the story of heaven's hound pursuing a woman discarded by all societal norms, and the tension that resulted as she worked the Fourth Step.

THE HOUND OF HEAVEN

In John 4, Jesus shifted his field of ministry from Judaea (to the south) to Galilee (to the north). In between lay the land of Samaria, whose citizens were the descendants of a generation of Jews who had intermarried with foreigners. In 720 B.C., the Assyrians invaded Israel's northern kingdom of Samaria. The Samaritans who were left behind soon began to intermarry with the Assyrians, and became known as half-Jews. Even centuries later, the people of Samaria were seen as the lowest of humanity, and the feud had yet to die down. The last place on earth you would find a Jewish man was in Samaria.

The trip ahead for Jesus and his band of disciples would be extended from three to six days if he went around Samaria. But the Scripture actually says "he had to go through Samaria" (John 4:4). Why? It wasn't because his chosen route was more convenient.

It was because Jesus is the Hound of Heaven.

Jesus stopped at Jacob's well, which had great memories for the Jewish people. Then he sent his disciples on ahead to buy food at a local Samaritan store. He would wait at the 100-foot well in the heat of the day with no bucket with which to draw water. Why?

Because Jesus is the Hound of Heaven.

Enter one Samaritan woman from the town of Sychar. She was a half-mile from home, meaning she was too much an outcast to draw water from her own town. Then Jesus broke all the societal rules when he (a) traveled through Samaria; (b) spoke to a woman, even though he was a rabbi; (c) spoke to a Samaritan woman; and (d) spoke to a Samaritan woman of ill repute. Why?

Because Jesus is the Hound of Heaven.

What Jesus did then, he continues today. No matter your addiction, how far you have fallen, or the definition of your "bottom," Jesus is pursuing you with all the forces from above. Why?

Because Jesus is the Hound of Heaven.

CAVERNOUS VOID

The Samaritan "came to draw water" (John 4:7). This led to a back-and-forth for the ages.

Jesus: "Will you give me a drink?"

Woman: "You are a Jew and I am a Samaritan woman. How can you ask me for a drink?"

Jesus: "If you knew the gift of God and who it is that asks you for a drink, you would have asked him and he would have given you living water."

Woman: "Where can you get this living water?"

Jesus: "Everyone who drinks this water will be thirsty again, but whoever drinks the water I give them will never thirst."

Woman: "Give me this water."

Many years ago, I was preaching at a church in Alabama. Just before the service began, I went down the hall for a drink of water. Over the drinking fountain was a plaque with these words: "Whoever drinks of this water shall thirst again."

The church was declaring the message of the cavernous void. The Samaritan woman had walked half a mile with a bucket in her hand, ready to lower that bucket 100 feet in order to get water. She had done the hard work. At last, in the heat of the day, she was on the cusp of finding water. Surely, the long journey, under the full sun, had left her with an enormous thirst. Yet, Jesus told her, there was a cavernous void between the well and living water.

Augustine said, "Our hearts are restless until they find rest in thee."[1] Walk into any 12-Step room and you will find men and women who are in search of this eternal rest. But too many exit the rooms with empty buckets. They do the work—walk a half mile in search of the water—but leave frustrated, unless they allow their Higher Power to fill their bucket. They leave with a cavernous void.

MORE THAN WATER

Jesus was there to talk about more than water. He changed subjects on a dime: "Go, call your husband and come back" (John 4:16). When the woman acknowledged she had no husband, Jesus said she had had five husbands and was currently living with a man outside of marriage.

Jesus was calling for a "searching, moral inventory" (Step Four). He called on her to list her character defects. Her inventory included five failed marriages and fornication.

It is a good thing to confess one's sin. But it is a better thing to confess one's sins. Name them. Lay them all out. Conduct a fearless inventory. You can't ask God to remove your character defects until you recognize what they are.

WILD GOOSE CHASE

Jesus suddenly shifted gears—again. On what must have felt like a wild goose chase to the Samaritan woman, he challenged her on the subject of worship. "You Samaritans worship what you do not know" (John 4:22). He added, "Those who worship the Father must worship in Spirit and truth" (John 4:23). Then he staked his claim as the Messiah.

What began as a simple journey in search of water evolved into a personal encounter with the living God. Their discussion bounced from water to living water to character defects to worship. What was Jesus really saying? I think it was clear—perhaps more to the woman than to us. "You must know your Higher Power." He was telling her (and us) that the real topic was not water, marriage, adultery, or divorce. It would not be hard to make the case that this woman was a sex or love addict. Therefore, when Jesus pointed her to true worship, he was really pointing her to true recovery.

To us he would say, "You can bring your bucket—personal effort, recovery literature, and sincere work—to the well. But that bucket won't hold water. Lay it down and come to me."

Sadly, we can do the work of recovery and not be recovered. That's because we must identify our character defects. And we must lay down our buckets and embrace a personal relationship with the Living Water.

OUR HIGHER POWER

In the AA "Big Book" we read these words: "Lack of power, that was our dilemma. We had to find a power by which we could live, and it had to be a *Power greater than ourselves*."[2] This was the essence of Jesus' unexpected encounter with the unsuspecting woman. She came with a bucket, but left with a well. It is when we lay our bucket down that our Higher Power can take over. We see four things about this power that is the topic of seven of the 12 steps. We see four attributes of Christ.

RELENTLESS

Francis Thompson was born the son of Catholic converts in England in 1859. But he did not embrace the faith of his parents. Through a series of major health challenges and bad personal choices, Thompson found himself destitute, living among the homeless of London, selling matches to raise enough money to buy food scraps on which to live.

But for young Francis, there was another battle raging in his life. It was a spiritual battle. He began to feel the relentless tug of God pulling on his heart. At the age of 34, he surrendered to this God, and then wrote a poem about his experience, titled *The Hound of Heaven*. The poem was immediately acclaimed as a masterpiece. Thompson would die eight years later, at the age of 42.

To the Samaritan woman, Jesus was the Hound of Heaven, relentless in his pursuit of her soul. That is why he "had to pass through Samaria." He did not walk that road to save three days' journey, but to save one woman's life. Know this—the same Hound of Heaven is hot on your trail. He is pursuing a relationship with you . . . a relationship that will secure your freedom from the chains that bind.

RELATIONAL

Jesus broke all the accepted norms of society when he talked to the woman of Samaria. He went to the wrong place at the wrong time with the wrong crowd to talk to the wrong person about the wrong things. Why did he do it? Because Jesus is all about relationships. Perhaps that's why Scripture records Jesus telling 35 short stories to 12 men but only one sermon to a large crowd. Perhaps that's why Jesus would stop on his way to raise a girl from the dead, in order to respond to the touch of a woman he'd never met. Perhaps that's why he locked eyes with Nicodemus and locked arms with Peter—knowing Peter would deny even knowing him. Perhaps that's why Jesus made time for little Zaccheaus and little children. Perhaps that's why men—seconds after being healed—always followed the same pattern—they wanted to be with Jesus.

Jesus is relational. He is more than a good story, a great rabbi, or a God-man. He is more than a messenger; he is the message. He saw the woman, he engaged the woman, he changed the woman. He seeks this same relationship with you. That is the foundation of recovery.

RESPECTFUL

God knocks on the door (Revelation 3:20). He does not kick it in. Jesus was respectful of the Samaritan woman. He didn't force the conversation or brow beat her over her character defects. He didn't force her to work the Fourth Step before she was ready. The woman was living with a man to whom she was not married. Nothing put her at odds with respected society more than that. But Jesus let her go first. She confessed her defects before Jesus offered a solution.

Bryant H. McGill, contributor for *USA Today* and the *Wall Street Journal*, wrote, "One of the sincerest forms of respect is actually listening to what another has to say."[3] Jesus captured the woman's heart be-cause she first captured his attention. Do you know someone who needs recovery? You can help—but only if you care about them even more than their *re-covery.*

REDEMPTIVE

Addiction recovery is not the ultimate goal. Jesus came to "seek and to save that which was lost" (Luke 19:10). He wanted to give the woman freedom—from her past, her mistakes, and her addictions. But there was one thing he wanted even more—her place in heaven. Her biggest defect was not five failed mar-riages or one inappropriate relationship. Her biggest problem, the one that threatened to ruin her life for eternity, was that she worshiped a God she did not know (John 4:22).

Chris Tomlin wrote, in *Jesus My Redeemer*, "You traded riches to run to my rescue, Oh, my redeemer. You take the pieces and turn them to praises, Oh, my redeemer."[4] That is what Jesus did for the woman of Samaria. He was—and will always be—the redemp-tive Christ.

CHARACTER DEFECTS

In 1944, Clarence Snyder wrote the pamphlet, *Going Through the Steps—A.A. Sponsorship Pamphlet.* In it, Snyder identified 20 specific character defects.[5]

When I first worked the Fourth Step, I discovered that I'm an overachiever; my defects could be counted by the dozen. We all have character defects, and most of us have a lot of them. The woman at the well had four obvious defects she needed to address in working her Fourth Step.

DISCONNECT FROM HIGHER POWER

This woman was so many of us. She had a complicated relationship with her higher power. She was interested, but not intimate; curious, but not connected. We see three expressions of her cluelessness. First, she had no idea what Jesus meant by "living water" (John 4:11). Second, the woman didn't understand true worship (John 4:21-24). Third, she failed to recognize the Messiah who was standing in front of her (John 4:25). The woman would have fit into American society seamlessly, with a form of godliness, but no power. Hers was an incomplete faith. She needed to make the real connection.

MULTIPLE MARRIAGES

We read an interesting dialogue between Jesus and this woman (John 4:16-18). Jesus said she had been married five times. For the record, U.S. Census surveys show that while 13% of Americans marry twice, only 3% marry a third time. The number who marry five times is about one in a thousand. This woman was an extreme example of failure in marriage. And that is precisely why Jesus made an example of her. He was sending a clear message for all generations to come—"If I can bring hope to a half-Jew, an outcast to society, a five-time failure, I can bring hope to you."

PARTIAL DISCLOSURE

The woman did what most of us do. It's what we call a partial disclosure. When Jesus told her to get her husband, she said she had no husband. Then Jesus pointed out that she had had five husbands and was currently living with a man to whom she was not married. Notice, she got no credit for that which she did disclose. Recovery requires *total* honesty, *total* transparency, *total* disclosure.

FORNICATION

Jesus said, "The fact is, you have had five husbands, and the man you now have is not your husband" (John 4:18). While it was merely implied that the woman had five divorces on her resume, this part is very clear. She was living with a man outside of marriage. In an article titled *The Science of Cohabitation* (published in *The Atlantic*, March 20, 2014), the authors revealed interesting data.[6] Two-thirds of couples live together before getting married. This is up 900% over the last 30 years. Further, those who cohabitate before marriage are 33% more likely to eventually divorce. Living together may be common—but that doesn't make it right—or healthy.

FOURTH STEP LESSONS

Let's bring it home. The woman at the well stands as a radiant example of what it takes to work the Fourth Step. Robert Frost said, "The best way out is always through." The 23rd Psalm promises God's presence through the valley, not out of it. Step Four is for those who are in the valley. It is not their ticket out, but through. Let's consider some examples of this critical Step in the story before us.

YOU MUST PASS THROUGH SAMARIA

"Now Jesus had to go through Samaria" (John 4:4). Samaria was the shortest route, but not the easiest. So it is with Step Four. It is the shortest route from Step Three to Step Five, but it's not easy. Most 12-Step literature contains a statement like this: "Rarely have we seen a person fail who has thoroughly followed our path. Those who do not recover are people who cannot or will not completely give themselves to this simple program of recovery."

It we could find recovery some other way, who wouldn't take that road? I mean, there are plenty of things that are more fun than brainstorming over one's character defects, writing them down, then talking about them with someone else. That is why, for so many, the Third Step becomes the final step. But that doesn't erase this critical truth about recovery—in order to get well, you must go through Samaria.

YOU NEED THE RIGHT SCORECARD

Working Step Four means talking about what you don't want to talk about. The woman was fine saying she was not married. But Jesus made her confront why she wasn't married. And Jesus pointed to her "bottom" behavior—living with a man outside of marriage, which was very rare in those days.

Writing out one's moral inventory can be exhausting. It generally starts with our resentments, such as resentments of people, organizations, and concepts. Then we list hurtful relationships: personal, sexual, and family. Then we write out our fears, such as rejection, abandonment, responsibility, pain, and the unknown. Many sponsors will have their sponsees include other categories in their inventories, such as self-centeredness, shame, and guilt. Working this step requires a guide who knows the right scorecard.

YOU CAN'T WORK STEP FOUR UNTIL YOU WORK STEP THREE

Process matters. Until you finish high school, you can't go to college. Until you get a driver's license, you can't drive a car. And until you complete Step Three, you can't work Step Four. Until you have "made a decision to turn your will and life over to the care of God as you understand him," you can't do an introspective inventory of yourself. You must get right with God before you can get right with yourself.

YOU CAN ACE YOUR HOMEWORK AND STILL FAIL THE COURSE

The woman at the well was religious. She knew her Old Testament history. She was looking for the coming Messiah. She was committed to worship. She had at least a rudimentary understanding of God. She had done all her homework, but still failed the course.

In recovery, you can read all the right books, attend all the right meetings, and say all the right things, and still fall short. I once knew a man who had attended three SAA meetings a week for 15 years. But I never knew him to have more than two weeks of sobriety. You can check all the boxes and still live in captivity to your most repulsive urges. You can ace your homework and still fail the course.

YOU MUST COME CLEAN TO GET CLEAN

John Piper said, "Jesus reveals sins to expose the thirst that we don't even know we have."[7] That is exactly what happened that afternoon by Jacob's well. The Samaritan woman knew she was thirsty, but she didn't realize she was thirsty.

Until the woman admitted her past she couldn't embrace her future. James said, "Humble yourselves in the sight of the Lord, and he will lift you higher" (James 4:10). God is more than willing to humble you, but it is when you humble yourself (come clean on your own) that you get well.

When a person attends his first 12-Step meeting he is told, "You don't need to admit to an addiction. Just state your first name." But that quickly changes. From meeting #2 on, you will be expected to introduce yourself as an addict. This is not to demean you, nor does it mean you are defined by your behavior. The point is simple. You must acknowledge that you are not well in order to get well. You must come clean in order to get clean.

It's called working the Fourth Step.

STEP FIVE

THE LEPER

MATTHEW 8:1-4

"We admitted to God, to ourselves, and to another human being the exact nature of our wrongs."

An old man burst into a priest's study and said, "I've got to confess right now. I'm 50 years old and have been faithful to my wife for the entirety of our 30-year marriage. Then, this gorgeous young lady moved in next door and began to flirt with me. Before I knew what had happened, I broke every command you can name."

"How long has it been since your last confession?" asked the priest.

"I've never been to confession," the man responded.

"Then may I ask why not?"

"It's simple. I'm Jewish."

The priest was startled. He asked, "Then why are you telling me all this?"

The sinner explained, "I'm telling everyone."

The Fifth Step tells us we need to tell someone our wrongs—not everyone, but someone. Lou Holtz said it like this: "When we fumble due to sin—and it's gonna happen—confession puts us back on the field." And Augustine said, "The confession of evil works is the beginning of good works."

JESUS' FIFTH STEP ENCOUNTER A SHORT STORY

The story before us (Matthew 8:1-4) is the shortest and most obscure of any of the 12-Step encounters of Christ. But it proclaims the powerful Fifth Step message of admitting our defects to God, self, and others. Here's the setting. Jesus had just delivered the greatest sermon ever heard, known as the Sermon on the Mount. Then it got interesting.

For over 30 years as a lead pastor, I preached as many as five weekend services. When I was done, I was *done*. After church, we rarely went to lunch with friends. We went straight home, ate lunch, watched sports, and took a nap. (When golf was on, I could watch sports and nap at the same time.)

But when Jesus was done, He was just getting started. As he came down off the mountain, the crowds stayed with Him. Then, of all the rich, famous, religious, and powerful men in the crowd, Jesus was drawn to a leper—the one man in the crowd who no one else would touch. And then a great healing unfolded almost as if to set the template for AA when they would write Step Five a few centuries later. In this passage, we find two parts to the Fifth Step.

PART ONE—"We admitted"

That's where it begins. In working Step Four we made a list of our character defects. We identified the nature of our wrongs. In Step Five we admit them. And that's a big step. It's one thing to acknowledge a wrong, but so much more to admit to it openly.

The unnamed leper in this story was not long-winded. He worked the Fifth Step in just ten words: "Lord, if you are willing, you can make me clean" (Matthew 8:2). Actually, we see Steps One-Four here, as well. With one short statement, the man (a) admitted that he was powerless and his life was unmanageable, (b) acknowledged that a Power greater than himself could make it right, (c) decided to turn his life and will over to God, (d) took an honest inventory of himself, and (e) admitted it to God and to others.

He admitted his leprosy, weakness, and inadequacy. Finally, after decades of enduring the most gruesome, hideous skin disease known to man, his moment of healing had come. He was ready to work the Fifth Step. He admitted.

PART TWO—"To God, ourselves, and to another human being"

First, he admitted his need to God. That was the first word out of his mouth—"Lord." The word means "boss." This was a sign of surrender. The man knew who his Higher Power was. Let me emphasize a few words: "**Lord**, if **you** are willing, **you** can make me clean." We must confess our sins *to God*. We must come clean *before* God. It is paramount that we admit it all to God. The order matters. Before we admit our flaws to anyone else (even ourselves), we are to admit them to God. That's how the Fifth Step says it. And that is how the leper did it.

Second, he admitted his need to himself. We see this more in his actions than his words. Notice that the leper was among the crowd who heard the great sermon. He immersed himself into a crowd that would not touch him nor likely even speak to him. He was seen as the most abased among them, rejected and condemned by God. They associated his disease with personal choice, followed by God's judgment, as with Miriam, Gehazi, and Uzziah. He must have been a leper because of something he had done wrong. For him to admit his condition to himself was to accept all of the societal consequences associated with it.

Third, he admitted his condition to another human being. Of course, his disease was in full view, for anyone to see. But Jesus told him to show himself to the priest after he was healed [more on that later]. This presumed the priest had prior knowledge of the man's condition. Thus, the poor leper met the conditions of Step Five. He admitted to God, himself, and at least one other human being the exact nature of his condition.

OTHER FIFTH-STEPPERS WHO MET JESUS

The obscure leper is not the only example of a living Fifth-stepper who encountered Jesus. One could argue that every person who got well worked this Step in the process. The Fifth Step is too integral a part of any man's recovery to be skipped over. Let's take a quick look at just a few examples.

OLD ST. NIC

He is the man who inspired the most famous words of Jesus: "For God so loved the world that he gave his only begotten son, that whoever believes in him should not perish, but have everlasting life" (John 3:16). But Nicodemus was much more than an extra in the background of a grand play.

Nicodemus was a Jew. More than that, he was a Pharisee. And more than that, he was a member of the Sanhedrin. His life after he met Jesus would become so significant that Nicodemus would be venerated by the Eastern Orthodox Church, the Roman Catholic Church, and the Anglican Church. He would have feasts named in his honor.

But first, he worked the Fifth Step. By coming to Jesus under the cloud of darkness, he was admitting a problem beyond his control. He had religion void of relationship and position void of peace. When Jesus explained his need to be "born again" (John 3:5, 7), St. Nic responded as a child: "How can this be?" (John 3:9). Nicodemus had a lot, but never enough—until he met Jesus.

SAD DAD

I have answered to quite a few titles in my time: Reverend, Pastor, Dr., Chaplain, Chairman, President (of small companies, not the United States). The two best titles are, of course, Husband and Dad. But I've got one with a really special meaning—Coach.

When my son was a kid, he played baseball. He was pretty good. And at every game, I was not in the stands, but on the field. I was a coach. I couldn't throw well or bat at all. But I was a coach. There were two reasons—the team was desperate, and I wanted to be with my son.

I've said it for years. When I die, here's what I want on my tombstone: "He coached his son's Little League team."

Whenever my son played—baseball or drums—I was there. I love my son more than life itself. That is why I can identify with the man in Mark 9. His son was demon possessed. I'm sure he had tried it all—doctors, prayers, crazy potions. Now it was time to try Jesus. He found the Great Physician and said, "Teacher, I brought you my son, who is possessed by a spirit" (Mark 9:17). Then he pled, "Help me overcome my unbelief!" (Mark 9:24).

The man admitted a problem beyond his control. He admitted it to himself, to God, and to others. He worked Step Five. And his son was healed.

OUT OF OPTIONS

We read her story in Mark 5. "A woman was there who had been subject to bleeding for twelve years. She had suffered a great deal under the care of many doctors and had spent all she had, yet instead of getting better she grew worse" (Mark 5:25-27). Sick. Broke. Hopeless. A sadder story was never told.

Now out of options, the woman played her final card. "When she heard about Jesus, she came up behind him in the crowd and touched his cloak, because she thought, 'If I just touch his clothes, I will be healed.' Immediately, her bleeding stopped and she felt in her body that she was freed from her suffering" (Mark 5:28-30).

Step One? Check. Step Two? Check. Step Three? Check. Step Four? Check. Step Five? CHECK!

CRIMINAL MINDS

On the day that Jesus died, he wasn't the only one on a cross. On one side was an unrepentant thief; on the other side, the criminal who would be saved. The repentant criminal rebuked the other: "Don't you fear God? We are punished justly" (Luke 23:40-41).

Then he turned to Jesus with a simple request: "Jesus, remember me when you come into your kingdom" (Luke 23:42). Moments before his death, he received this promise: "Today, you will be with me in paradise" (Luke 23:43).

Even a criminal mind can be saved if he works the Fifth Step. The repentant thief admitted his flaws and reached out to Jesus. The next words he would speak would be spoken to Jesus as well—this time in paradise.

DOUBTING THOMAS

Scene 1—The resurrected Jesus appeared to the disciples. Thomas was not there.

Scene 2—The others told Thomas, who said he'd believe only if he touched the wounds of Christ himself.

Scene 3—A week later, Jesus appeared again. This time, Thomas was there. Jesus offered for Thomas to touch his side. Thomas declined.

Scene 4—Thomas confessed, "My Lord and my God!"

You can read the story for yourself in the 20th chapter of the Gospel of John. At first, Thomas thought he didn't need the other disciples in his life. He moved on. But it wasn't long before he came to admit that he was running on empty. So he came back to the group—and to Jesus. What a life-changing moment that must have been. History tells us that the man who entered the room as Doubting Thomas would exit the room a missionary who committed the next 40 years of his life to evangelizing the lost in foreign lands. He would eventually be the final apostle put to death for his faith. Thomas lived and died by Step Five.

THE ONE THAT GOT AWAY

He's the answer to a great Bible trivia question—name the only man in Scripture who walked away from Jesus sad. His story is found in Mark 10:17-22. He is known as the rich young ruler. And he started out well. Notice all he did right. The man (a) ran to Jesus, (b) fell on his knees before Him, (c) called Him "good teacher," and (d) lived a largely righteous life.

When he came to Jesus, he brought this question with him: "What must I do to inherit eternal life?" And he apparently didn't like the answer. When Jesus told him to give away his wealth (surrender), "the man's face fell and he went away sad" (Mark 10:22). The young leader demonstrated the difference between interest and commitment, half-hearted measures and recovery. He failed to admit the exact nature of his wrongs. The result? He flunked the Fifth Step. He was the one who got away.

FIVE THEMES OF EVERY FIFTH STEP

Working Step Five is one tough challenge—especially for men. It's one thing to write out our character flaws with the help of our sponsor (Step Four). It's something entirely different to share this with others, even God. Steven Arterburn offers valuable insight. After conducting a survey of 3,600 men, he wrote *The Secrets Men Keep*.[1] Among his findings were two interesting facts. First, men want to be respected even more than they want to be loved. And second, 85% of Christian men feel disrespected. So what does this have to do with Step Five? Everything! Men are reticent to confess their struggles out of fear—specifically, a fear of losing respect.

A civil war ensues. On one side is the security of personal respect. On the other side is reality. The problem is that reality involves risk. It means being known. Fear often takes over. The only answer is to work the Fifth Step. And that is exactly what the leper did (Matthew 8). The same was true of our other examples.

When studying the cases of each of these Fifth-steppers, we unveil five themes throughout.

EACH HAD A PROBLEM BEYOND HIS CONTROL.

I love the Great Initiator. In our primary story, Jesus initiated the action. He saw the leper before the leper saw him. And while tradition held that a person was never to touch a leper (lest he catch the deadly disease), Jesus did it anyway. While the labor of his day dictated that Jesus needed rest, he went to the man anyway. And while no rabbi would even think about associating so closely with a leper, Jesus did it anyway.

Jesus knew the trauma that was at the root of this man's insecurity. He knew how hard it was for the man to simply show up. The leper's life was one of abject isolation. Lepers were beggars, loners, and the outcasts of outcasts. And this isolation makes a leper—get ready to be offended—much like you and me.

We read in the AA Big Book, "Almost without exception, alcoholics are tortured by loneliness."[2] The same is true of all addicts. We live in isolation and loneliness. It's a horrible place to live. I know because I've been there.

Each of the men and women we have covered had a problem beyond their control. They all knew it. And each one—except the rich young ruler—was ready to do something about it. And that is each of us. We all have our own form of leprosy. We try to maintain control, but we are out of control. Only when we admit that can we become well.

EACH REFUSED TO MINIMIZE HIS PROBLEM.

When preaching in a church not long ago, I made this statement: "I will help any man who is mired in addiction—except one. I will not, and cannot help the man who is not truly desperate." For most of us, we have to dig a hole, then keep digging for years, before we are ready to do whatever it takes to crawl out. It takes a lot for us to get desperate. Until then, we acknowledge the problem, but we minimize it. Men are especially gifted at the art of minimization.

There is something I've noticed about human nature. We tend to judge others by their actions, but we judge ourselves by our intentions. But here's a newsflash. "Intending to stop acting out" isn't the same thing as "stopping acting out."

This isn't to say the addict chose his malady any more than the leper chose leprosy. There was a common assumption in that day that lepers were that way because of bad behavior or unwise choices. They were sick because of something they had done. Of course, that was wrong. And it is also wrong to assume addicts became who they are by bad choices. The fact is, addiction is rooted in isolation, abuse, and trauma, not choice. But *living* in that addiction is a choice. And when we quit minimizing, we start to get well.

EACH BROUGHT HIS ISSUE TO JESUS.

Every 12-Step group speaks of a "Higher Power." Personally, I am perfectly comfortable in my own recovery, attending a meeting that is "secular," in the sense that it does not adopt a Christological approach. I know who my Higher Power is, and I speak about Him openly in and out of meetings. But I am fine with non-believers attending our meetings. I'm glad they do.

But when Beth and I work with clients, we make no apology for our adherence to Jesus Christ as our

Higher Power. We certainly don't force our beliefs on anyone. But it is impossible to be a Christ-follower who respects the tenets of Scripture, and also be a universalist. In other words, I cannot accept nor promote a cafeteria-style approach to finding God.

The leper came to Jesus. Nicodemus came to Jesus. The father came to Jesus. The woman came to Jesus. The thief on the cross came to Jesus. Thomas came to Jesus. Even the rich young ruler came to Jesus.

Here's why it matters. If we really believe recovery cannot be accomplished apart from God, we need to know who God is. I know guys who make their SA group their "Higher Power." But postmodern, "pick your god, any god" thinking doesn't alter the identity of the real God. To complete Step Five successfully, you must admit your problem to God, not god.

EACH CAME WITH DESPERATION.

None of our Fifth-stepper friends came casually. There was an urgency with each one. Imagine the leper. He followed Jesus to the mountain to hear the great sermon. Then he followed him away, amidst the pressing crowd. Then, even though he was surely pushed aside for his leprosy, he somehow managed to get close. "He came and knelt before Jesus" (Matthew 8:2). This took a lot of determination.

In 1977, I saved my money so I could buy two tickets to a Johnny Cash concert in Houston. My girlfriend liked Johnny Cash more than she liked me, so this was a great opportunity. I managed to buy two tickets on the end of the row, next to the aisle Cash would walk down on the way to the stage, which was in the round, in the middle of the arena. Sure enough, my date and I were able to reach out and touch Johnny and June Carter Cash as they passed by.

Here's the good news for any addict. You can touch Jesus if you want it badly enough. If the woman with the issue of blood could get to Jesus, so can you. If the father with the sick son could get to Jesus, so can you. But you have to be desperate.

EACH LIVED OUT HIS LIFE IN COMMUNITY.

The story of the leper ended curiously. Jesus told the man to not let anyone know of his healing—yet. First, he was to find the priest and show him. Why?

A man was not considered healed from a disease such as leprosy until the priest certified him as "well." And until the leper had received that official report from the priest, he could not re-engage in society, get a job, or even touch another human being. Jesus was respecting the law, while watching out for the man's best interests at the same time.

By instructing the man to go before a priest, he was preparing the way for the man to live the rest of his life in community. That is a part of Step Five—"Admit to God, yourself, *and to another human being* the exact nature of your wrongs."

One of the most profound verses of the New Testament is found in the Book of James. We are told, "Confess your sins to one another and pray for one another, that you may be healed" (James 5:16). Notice that we are not told to confess our sins to God, but to each other. While it is a given that we must confess to God, James is telling us that this is not enough. We are to live in community. And that doesn't happen until we get real with one another.

Patrick Carnes has created an interesting exercise that helps. In *Facing the Shadows*, he recommends an exercise he calls an "Important People Inventory."[3] In this exercise, the addict makes a list of those with whom he will share his struggles. How you share your struggles with others isn't the point; just make sure that you do. Become a Fifth-stepper. Admit to God, yourself, and another human being the exact nature of your wrongs.

STEP SIX

THE PARALYTIC

JOHN 5:1-15

"We were entirely ready to have God remove all these defects of character."

Two years before his death, Bill W., co-founder of Alcoholics Anonymous, published his final work, written for men and women working through their Sixth and Seventh Steps of recovery. I have found this book, *Drop the Rock*, to be of great value for clients who have completed their Fourth Step inventory and are ready to separate themselves from the defects that have held them back.

The premise of *Drop the Rock* is based on a simple story. A man is on a boat with his friends, then somehow slips and falls overboard. As the boat moves away, he struggles to get back on the boat, but can't quite make it. He fights to stay above water, but finds himself going under. He suddenly realizes that around his neck is a chain with a giant rock, a burden too heavy with which to swim. His friends yell out, "Drop the rock! Drop the rock!" At first, he resists, because as crazy as it seems, he kind of likes the rock.

Soon, the man realizes he can't have it both ways. He must choose life or death, the boat or the rock. In a last gasp of desperation, he releases the rock. This frees him to swim to the boat, where he finds safety.

The rock represents character defects. In traditional AA literature, the focus is on fear, anger, and resentments. For our purposes, the rock represents any flaw related to our addiction—or the addiction itself.

AA calls Step 6 "the step that separates the men from the boys."[1] The problem is that while the addict is to be congratulated for completing the first five Steps, he has not been asked (by the Steps) to actually give anything up quite yet. Even this Step makes no real demands of him. But it moves him closer, beyond the point of turning back.

The key word is "entirely." The reason most of us are not *entirely* ready to surrender our defects to God is that we are more comfortable with a problem we see than a solution we don't. Our addiction has become our most reliable friend. It is there any time we need it, available at a moment's notice. When our wife, husband, kids, job, or any other person or circumstance seem to turn against us, it is there. When we are lonely, it is there. I get it; I've been there. In the moment, it's not hard to make the argument for a quick fix "just one more time." We know we shouldn't indulge, but we reason it's "just one more time."

Substitute the word *desperate* for *entirely ready*. We'll understand that more fully as we dig into John 5. Jon Bloom, co-founder of *Desiring God*, said it well. "The lack of a sense of desperation for God is deadly."[2] But if you are ready—truly desperate—you can find the peace and recovery that have eluded you for too long.

JESUS' SIXTH STEP ENCOUNTER THE GREATEST HEALING STORY OF ALL-TIME

I know what you are probably thinking. "I've been this way most of my life." And it's true. You didn't ask to see your dad's porn stash when you were six years old. You didn't ask for the emotional abuse you suffered at the hands of disconnected parents. You certainly didn't sign up for the trauma and isolation that fed your early addiction.

I have a friend who struggled in his addiction his entire life, until two years ago. He didn't know what it was like to go 30 days without sexual self-gratification, the use of pornography, and a litany of other acting out behaviors. Then something changed. Two years ago, he became entirely ready. In his desperation, he worked the Sixth Step—and more. And now my friend has been completely sober and free for two years.

My friend is 93.

In this week's 12-Step encounter, we find Jesus with a man who had struggled in his pain and helplessness for 38 years. We read his story in the fifth chapter of the fourth Gospel. Allow me to paraphrase that story.

One day, Jesus went to Jerusalem for a religious feast. Approaching his destination, he passed by a pool called Bethesda, which was thought to provide healing powers to those who could make their way to the water's edge. It was therefore not unexpected that Jesus would come upon any number of sufferers—the blind, lame, and paralyzed.

One of the men Jesus saw had been an invalid for 38 years. This was the day that would change everything. What happened next can happen for you—or anyone who is *entirely ready* to be healed. Every healing, every successful working of the Sixth Step, follows the same predictable pattern. We see four conditions that must be met.

DESIRE (John 5:1-6)

"Jesus saw him lying there and learned that he had been in this condition for a long time" (John 5:6). I love that. Jesus was the interruptible Christ. On His way to an important Jewish festivity, He saw the man lying on the side of the road. Instinct might have kicked in. "I have someplace to be. This guy is with others just like him. He's made it this far. I'll check on him after my important event."

But the interruptible one couldn't let it go. When Jesus saw him, it was over. Jesus was the Son of God, the second person of the trinity. But there was one thing that He struggled to do. He seemed almost incapable of seeing someone in need and just walking away. Jesus saw him. Then He spoke to him.

What followed was the most unusual question in the Bible.

"Do you want to be well?" (John 5:6).

Was that a serious question? Of course the man wanted to be well, right? Actually, this is not a given. You see, the word for "want" implied desperation. Jesus was asking, "Do you *really* want to be well?" And that's a huge difference.

Teddy Roosevelt famously said, "When you come to the end of your rope, tie a knot and hang on!" Bad advice. But that is what most of us do. When you come to the end of the rope, what do you do? The problem with tying a knot and hanging on is that this implies self-effort. You didn't get into the mess you're in because of lack of effort. It was lack of surrender that got you here.

If you sort of want to be well, you'll tie your own knot. But if you *really* want to be well, you will be entirely ready for God to take over.

Take a break and ask yourself that question. "Do I want to be well—really?" Until you register a reading of "Absolute Desperation" on your desire meter, you will not get well.

OBEDIENCE (John 5:7-8)

Martin Lloyd-Jones said, "Love is not just a sentiment. Love is a great controlling passion and it always expresses itself in terms of obedience."[3] We need to resurrect the old hymn: "Trust and obey. Trust and obey. For there's no other way to be happy in Jesus— but to trust and obey."

Jesus asked the paralytic if he *really, really* wanted to be well. Satisfied with his response, Jesus moved to the next level. "Jesus said to him, 'Get up! Pick up your mat and walk.' And the man was cured; he picked up his mat and walked" (John 5:7-8).

Notice the process. Until the man was willing to do the improbable, Jesus would not do the impossible. Jesus told him to pick up his mat (improbable) and walk (impossible).

Then the Bible tells us that "the man was cured." But he still hadn't walked. His next move was to pick up his mat. That was something he could actually do without walking. Of course, there wouldn't be much point. The man was still trying to drag himself to the water. So why would he pick up his mat *before* walking? As far as he knew, he wasn't yet cured. While he had received the healing, he did not actually experience the healing until he took a step of obedience. Once he did what he could do, Jesus did what He could do.

Dwight L. Moody said, "God doesn't seek for golden vessels, and does not ask for silver ones, but he must have clean ones."[4] When we really want it, and are obedient to do whatever it takes, we can get well.

DISCLOSURE (John 5:10-13)

Religious leaders can be such downers! When the Jewish leaders heard the man had been gloriously healed—after 38 years—did they (a) rejoice in the goodness of God, or (b) pout that the man picked up his mat on the Sabbath Day? You guessed it. They were more absorbed with process than results. Never mind that the Bible actually never did forbid this level of "work" on the Sabbath. They found some obscure extra-biblical rule that did, and that was good enough for them.

When they interrogated the man, he confessed he knew little about Jesus or their stupid laws. He could only say, "The man who made me well said to me, 'Pick up your mat and walk'" (John 5:11). It's the first part that mattered: "The man who made me well."

In recovery, when you are made well, you need to tell somebody. In 12-Step work, this is called "doing the First Step." In therapy, it is a clinical disclosure. Dr. Milton Magness defines it like this: "Disclosure is a clinical procedure that takes place only after preparation of both the sex addict and the partner, and is guided by a well-trained sex addiction therapist as part of the treatment process" (*Stop Sex Addiction*, p. 99).

COMMUNITY (John 5:14-15)

Recovery is a team sport. Notice how the story ends. "Later Jesus found him at the temple and said to him, 'See, you are well again. Stop sinning or something worse may happen to you.' The man went away and told the Jewish leaders that it was Jesus who had made him well" (John 5:14-15).

There's a lot to unpack in these two verses. Jesus said he was "well again." This implies that he had been well before. Apparently, prior to his 38-year affliction, he could walk. One can only imagine how he became lame or the emotions that had flooded his soul for a generation.

Jesus warned him, "Stop sinning or something worse may happen to you" (John 5:14). Our personal behaviors (sins/addictions) can bring more trauma and pain than the inability to even walk.

Finally, we see the man telling the Jewish leaders that it was Jesus who had made him well. His disclosure was now complete, and he would step into an incredible future with a pretty cool testimony.

But I want to focus on the first part of these verses. "Later Jesus found him at the temple." This is a powerful statement. Jesus never told him to go to "church," but he went anyway. There was something deep inside the man that screamed out for fellowship and support. He didn't know how he knew it, but he knew it. Intuitively, he was compelled to get into community as soon after his healing as possible.

WHERE WE GET OFF THE RAILS WITH STEP SIX

A character flaw can be a good thing if we let it point us to God. Tim Keller said, "The more you see your own flaws and sins, the more precious, electrifying, and amazing God's grace appears to you."[5] In working Step Six, remember those two words: *entirely ready*. Bill W. said, "I don't get to choose which defects God will remove." The step seems clear. The wording is not ambiguous. The bar is high, but the instructions are easy to read. Still, many flail aimlessly and unsuccessfully at this point. We create our own versions of Step 6 in order to map an easier course. In so doing, we get off the rails in three ways. These are our personal, preferred alternatives to Step Six.

WE WERE PARTIALLY READY.

Many of us are mostly ready to dig deep into recovery. But we want the results without the process. We want the blessings without the pain. We are like a couple in the New Testament. Acts 5 records the story of Ananias and Sapphira.

This early church couple was ready to do whatever was needed—almost. We find the early church committed to sharing their possessions (voluntarily) with one another for the common good. As an example, Barnabas sold a plot of land and then donated the entire proceeds to the apostles.

Following this example, Ananias and Sapphira sold their property, then gave the donation to Peter. But they did not give it all. "Ananias kept back part of the money for himself" (Acts 5:2). It could be argued that Ananias and Sapphira did more than most, because they gave a large portion of their proceeds to others. But partial obedience is disobedience.

Peter was certainly not impressed with their gift. He asked, "Why is it that Satan has so filled your heart that you have lied to the Holy Spirit?" (Acts 5:3). He accused them of dishonesty, as they sought praise for that which they did not give. (Note: God is more impressed with how little we keep than with how much we give.) It wasn't long before both fell dead, under the judgment of God.

Andrew Murray wisely said, "God is ready to assume full responsibility for the life wholly yielded to him."[6] I work with so many men who are partially, even mostly, ready. I want to drag them over the finish line. But that is a line they must cross for themselves.

WE WERE TEMPORARILY READY.

Jesus told the story of the farmer who went out to sow some seed (Luke 8). We read four results from the seed: (a) some fell along the path and was eaten by the birds; (b) some fell on rocky soil and the growth was short-lived for lack of moisture; (c) some fell among thorns and was choked; (d) some fell on good soil and yielded a bountiful crop.

Our interest is with the second example. "Those on the rocky ground are the ones who receive the word with joy when they hear it, but they have no root. They believe for a while, but in the time of testing they fall away" (Luke 8:13).

This is the most accurate picture of a 12-Step meeting you'll find. The rocky soil represents the empty chair many groups set in the middle of the room before meetings. This is done in remembrance of the man or woman who has dabbled in recovery, but is not yet ready to go all in.

I have phone numbers for about 50 men I've met in recovery. They are stored in my phone, mostly under false names. But when I recently looked through my contact list, I was humbled to discover that I don't even remember half of these guys. So how did I get their first names and cell numbers? It's simple. They came to a few meetings, seemed to go all in, and in some cases, even asked me to be their sponsor. But soon, they faded. Some of them can't be found with a search warrant. They began showing up at meetings, seeming to be all in. But it didn't last. Instead of being entirely ready, they were just temporarily ready. The seed fell on rocky soil.

WE WERE ALMOST READY.

We get off the rails with Step Six when we are partially ready or temporarily ready to have God remove our shortcomings. But there is a third group. It's probably the largest of all. I see these guys all the time. They are *almost* ready. They are King Agrippa.

Agrippa was a king over the region of Judea from 41 to 44 A.D. He was a friend to Jews but antagonistic toward Christians. He was vigorous in his suppression of the upstart movement, for fear of its threat to his government. And then he met Paul, who presented a dilemma. Paul's Jewish credentials were unimpeachable. But he was also a proclaimer of "the way," or early Christianity.

The encounter of Agrippa and Paul was legendary. Paul made the most convincing case for Christ that anyone could imagine. Following Paul's final arguments, Agrippa responded, "Do you think that in such a short time you can persuade me to be a Christian?" (Acts 26:28). I love the way the old King James Version has it: "Thou almost persuadest me to become a Christian."

Almost persuaded—the last words of too many dying men. Those are also the unspoken words of millions of men and women who have wandered into a 12-Step meeting, listened to the stories of others, read some material . . . then walked away.

"Jeff" was a good friend. He came to about ten meetings. He heard our stories. He knew he needed what we had. He was so close. But he couldn't buy into the whole "Higher Power" thing. He eventually left us. The last I heard, he was arrested for transporting child pornography across state lines. Sadly, Jeff was *almost persuaded.*

"Ian" was in and out of meetings for three or four years. He'd come for a while, then disappear. He kept coming back—but he didn't last. He liked what he heard, but he never quite embraced it for himself. And now, he has lost his marriage. Sadly, Ian was *almost persuaded.*

"Jose" jumped right in. By his second SA meeting, he had purchased all the literature, entered counseling, and started his step work. But he never embraced accountability. He was afraid of being really known, so he never got a sponsor. He didn't last in recovery. The last I heard, Jose was back on the streets, spending every dollar he has on prostitutes. Someone said they heard he contracted an STD. Sadly, Jose was *almost persuaded.*

WRAP-UP

Dwight L. Moody famously preached, "Let God have your life; he can do more with it than you can." Moody was arguing for the Sixth Step, though the Steps would not be "invented" for another 50 years. Jesus is all about the 12 Steps. This is not clearer in any step more than the Sixth. It is only when we become "entirely ready to have God remove these defects of character" that true sobriety can come.

There is an old story about the pastor who longed to see an outpouring of God's power upon his church.

One night he had a dream. In his dream, an angel approached him with an empty key ring. The angel explained, "I have been sent by God. He has instructed me to collect from you the key to every room of your life."

The man gladly obliged the angel's request, reaching into his heart and pulling out dozens of keys. He carefully placed each key on the angel's key ring. At that, the angel departed.

A little later in the pastor's dream, the angel returned—with the key ring still filled with keys. The angel handed the entire key ring over to the man, with each key still in its place.

"But I offered these keys to God," the man explained. "Why are you returning them?"

The angel replied, "God has told me that you are hanging onto one key, which opens one more door in your heart."

"But it's just one key," the pastor protested.

"I'm sorry, it's all or none," explained the angel.

After several moments, the pastor acquiesced, reaching deep into his heart for what he thought would be the most insignificant key of all. But what he discovered was a key that was large, dirty, and rusted. The angel wanted it anyway.

The pastor released his final key. Shortly thereafter, he awoke, with the dream still very vivid in his mind.

He got the message. The next morning, he became *entirely ready* to give it all over to God. Soon after, his church experienced a revival on a scale never seen in her illustrious past.

What about you? You have identified your defects (Step Four) and have confessed them to God, yourself, and one other person (Step Five). Now, are you ready to surrender them to God? Here's a better question . . .

Are you entirely ready?

STEP SEVEN

THE CENTURION'S SON

LUKE 7:1-10
"We humbly asked God to remove our shortcomings."

Confucius said, "Humility is the foundation of all virtues." That is what Step Seven is all about— humbly coming before God. Robert Hemfelt wrote, "Although Step Seven is the shortest step in terms of wording and is perhaps the least discussed in recovery groups, it is probably the most potent of the twelve. It embodies the miracle of transformation as we turn over to God our broken, defective personalities in order that he might mold them into healthy, effective instruments of his will."[1]

Whereas Step Six calls for readiness, the Seventh Step calls for action. The addict has identified his shortcomings (Step Four), shared his shortcomings (Step Five), and prepared to do something about his shortcomings (Step Six). But none of that will do him much good unless he follows through with Step Seven.

Before turning to Jesus' next 12-Step encounter, let's consider an event in history, which perfectly depicts what happens when one man applies the principles of the Seventh Step to his personal life. Let me introduce you to a 48-year-old man named Jeremy.

JEREMY LANPHIER

It happened at lunchtime on September 23, 1857. Here's the background.

A Dutch Reformed church in lower Manhattan hired a layman named Jeremy Lanphier to start an aggressive visitation program to turn around the church's declining attendance. His honest efforts were met with dismal results, so Lanphier decided on a different strategy—prayer.

He rented a hall on Fulton Street and began handing out leaflets promoting the coming prayer gathering. Expecting a large crowd, Jeremy filled the hall with chairs. Sadly, only six people came. But what happened that day in 1857 would be just the beginning.

This small band of prayer warriors humbly sought God. They confessed their own sins and shortcomings before praying for anyone else. And then they prayed for something—anything necessary—to happen to return America to her spiritual roots. Within three weeks, the number of repentant prayer warriors had swelled from six to forty. And then their prayers were answered.

On October 10, 1857, the stock market crashed. People became desperate for help, and for God. Within six months, this prayer movement that began with one man, then six, had grown to 10,000. In February 1858, Gordon Bennett, of the New York Herald, began writing daily articles on the revival, which spread to St. Louis, Chicago, and Cleveland.

Unlike other great awakenings, this movement was not linked to powerful preaching nor was it tied to any famous leaders. The movement did not begin with an extraordinary sermon, a gifted theologian, or a big name such as Moody, Edwards, or Whitefield.

The movement began with one layman named Jeremy Lanphier, who did what the Seventh Step tells us all to do. He humbly asked God to remove his shortcomings.

JESUS' SEVENTH STEP ENCOUNTER
THE ROMAN CENTURION

THE STORY (Luke 7:1-10)

Jesus entered Capernaum, which had become his home base for ministry. The servant of a government official who lived nearby was gravely ill. This official only knew of Jesus by reputation. Luke says, "the centurion heard of Jesus" (Luke 7:3). The official sent word to Jesus to come heal his servant. The messengers reached Jesus and begged him to come heal the centurion's servant. Jesus agreed, and was led toward the home of the Roman official.

Then the story took a strange twist. When Jesus was nearing the house, He was met by friends of the centurion. They brought Him this message: "Lord, don't trouble yourself, for I do not deserve to have you come under my roof. That is why I did not even consider myself worthy to come to you. But say the word, and my servant will be healed" (Luke 7:6-7).

Jesus turned this into a teaching moment. With a crowd following Him, He turned to them and proclaimed, "I tell you, I have not found such great faith even in Israel" (Luke 7:9). With that, the centurion's friends returned home to find the servant healed.

THE CENTURION

When we learn more about the centurion, we are driven toward the tenets of the Seventh Step. Who was this man of humility and faith? A centurion was a Roman army officer in charge of 100 men. That meant he was a Gentile. How he heard of Jesus, we don't know. But we do know this—he clearly believed that Jesus was sent from God. With Capernaum as a part of his territory, perhaps he had heard enough of Jesus and his teachings/miracles to establish a faith in Him.

We also see that the centurion was a friend of the Jews. His first line of messengers said, "This man deserves to have you do this, because he loves our nation and has built our synagogue" (Luke 7:4-5). As

a Roman official, he couldn't have built a Jewish synagogue with government money; he must have done
this from his own resources.

Why did the centurion send Jewish elders to Jesus instead of going himself? There may have been
three reasons. First, he surely understood the cultur-
al dilemma. Jews hated Roman soldiers. Had he gone
personally, this might have created undue disruption
around Jesus and His ministry. Second, it was normal
for him, as an army captain, to delegate. This is what
he did all the time, as he made decisions on which
men would be sent into battle at particular times.
Third, perhaps he simply wanted to remain at the side
of his dying friend.

To summarize, we know a few things about this
man: (a) he was a Gentile, (b) he was a Roman official,
(c) he was in charge of over 100 Roman warriors, (d)
he was familiar with Jesus, (e) he demonstrated significant humility, and (f) he was a man of incredible
faith.

THE SERVANT

We read only that the man was dying. We don't
know his name, age, rank, or faith. But we can surmise
a few things. He must have been a good worker. The
centurion had established a rare attachment to him.
Of all the men who served under the centurion, plus all
of his other servants, this particular servant had stolen his heart. He risked his reputation as a Gentile by

reaching out to Jesus. He refused to leave his friend's side. This servant was clearly a man of character and reputation.

THE ELDERS

"The centurion heard of Jesus and sent some of the elders of the Jews to him, asking him to come and heal his servant. When they came to Jesus, they pleaded earnestly with him" (Luke 7:3-4).

Notice that while the centurion could have sent others among his personal servants (as he did when Jesus approached his home), he chose instead to send "Jewish elders." Why? There may have been two reasons.

First, as Jewish leaders, they might connect better with a Jewish rabbi (Jesus). The Roman leader may have sent them in order to establish his affinity for Jesus and the Jewish faith in the eyes of the great Healer.

Second, these elders would be the right messengers. Had the centurion's personal servants attested to his character and love for the synagogue, that might have appeared biased. But these Jewish elders, likely serving in the very synagogue the centurion had built, were the perfect messengers. If they could vouch for the man who was a (a) Roman, and (b) Gentile, this would confirm his character and the veracity of his request.

THE SAVIOR

I love Jesus' response. He listened to the plea of total strangers. His response was one of action, rather than words. "So Jesus went with them" (Luke 7:6). There was no hesitation. Jesus was a man driven by His desire to heal the sick, save the lost, and comfort the hurting. He didn't wait. As always, His timing was perfect.

Nearing the house, Jesus was met by a new posse. This time, He was approached by personal friends of the centurion. His message to Jesus was that he was not worthy to host Him, and a personal visit was unnecessary. Jesus could heal the sick man without even seeing him in the flesh, said the centurion. "Say the word, and my servant will be healed," he proclaimed (Luke 7:7).

Jesus didn't even need to "say the word." He praised the Roman official's faith, then turned to walk away. The servant was healed before the messengers had time to return home.

Anyone reading this amazing account should respond with a question. How can I get my prayers answered as surely as the centurion's prayers were answered? I suggest that in this story, we find two truths about the Savior.

First, He responds to needs. When He became aware of the critical nature of the need, Jesus responded right away. He is really into needs more than wants. Do you have any special needs in your life today—physical, financial, emotional, or spiritual? Take them to Jesus; He responds to needs.

Second, the Savior responds to faith. He commended the centurion's "great faith" (Luke 7:9). There are dozens of verses in the New Testament that confirm this. Faith moves mountains. Along with hope and love, it is the most critical trait to be cherished. Jesus responds to needs and He responds to faith. When both criteria are met, watch out! Jesus is up to something big!

FOUR PARTS TO THE SEVENTH STEP

It's the shortest step: "We humbly asked God to remove our shortcomings." That seems simple enough, right? Actually, there is a lot here to unpack. As we saw in Jesus' Seventh Step encounter, this is a step of action that calls for real courage. In working Step Seven, we put ourselves out there—relying on someone other than ourselves.

PART A: "HUMBLY"

Step Seven is about the person's perspective before it is about his action. The addict is not told to *pray humbly*, but to *humbly pray*. It's humility before prayer. Until he is right, his prayers won't be right. "The whole emphasis of Step Seven is on humility."[2]

It was humility that kept the centurion at home when he needed Jesus to heal his servant. It was humility that shaped Moses to be "very meek, more than all people who were on the face of the earth" (Numbers 12:3). It was humility that transformed the life of Paul, who said, "But what things were gain to me, these I counted loss for Christ" (Philippians 3:6). And it was humility that drove Jesus to the cross.

Tom Landry was one of the greatest coaches in NFL history. His gentle, Christian spirit was legendary. But his humility was on full display with the unveiling of his nine-foot statue at the Dallas Cowboys' new stadium. When Mrs. Landry was asked what she thought of the statue, she commented, "It's nice, but I always thought of Tom as being bigger than that." Everyone who knew Tom Landry felt that way about him. He was huge, because he was humble.

The prophet of old stated God's will for each of our lives. "He has shown you, all mortals, what is good. And what does the Lord require of you? To act justly and to love mercy and to walk humbly with your God" (Micah 6:8). That is quite the trifecta: (a) act justly, (b) love mercy, (c) walk humbly.

As a young pastor, I was blessed by the invitation to meet with Dr. Ed Young, pastor of Houston's Second Baptist Church (now the largest Southern Baptist Church in America). Dr. Young met with about 25 of us that evening—all young pastors in the Houston area. He gave a great talk on pastoral leadership, then fielded a series of questions. When it got late, he said we were free to leave, but any who wanted to stay were welcome to join him in his private office for pizza. There, he met with three of us past midnight.

It was a fantastic meeting with one of America's greatest church leaders. But I only remember one thing he said that night. When asked the key to effective leadership, Dr. Young said, "The first thing you have to learn to do, gentlemen, is walk on your knees." It was a lesson on humility. And it was a lesson that I needed to hear.

Rick Warren was right when he said, "Humility is not thinking less of yourself; it's thinking of yourself less."[3] If you are to complete the Seventh Step, that's how you will do it. It starts and ends on your knees. There is no other way.

PART B: "ASKED GOD"

The person must be right—*humility*. Then he must do the right thing—*ask God*. In Step Six we prepare to ask God to remove our shortcomings; now it's time to actually do it. So let's talk about prayer. What does it mean?

Billy Graham defined prayer in simple terms. "Prayer is simply a two-way communication with God."[4] About 150 years ago, Charles Spurgeon warned, "Prayer must be more than a vocal performance."[5] The disciples understood the need for prayer when they begged Jesus to teach them "to pray" (Matthew 6:5).

Let's break this part of the Seventh Step down a little more, taking it one word at a time.

The step says, *"We humbly asked God . . ."* The Scripture says, "You have not because you ask not" (James 4:3). Zig Ziglar used to say, "The biggest reason we don't get others to buy what we're selling is that we don't ask."[6]

The word James uses for "ask" means to implore. It brings the idea of passion and urgency. When we ask God to remove our shortcomings, we don't do so casually. The point is to pour ourselves out with the same energy and importance that would mark any prayer for our child's healing or for help in some other personal crisis.

The second word is equally critical. *"We humbly asked **God**."* At the risk of offending the broader 12-Step community, not just any "god" will do. I would be doing you a disservice if I said, "Find your own Higher Power. He, she, or it can be whomever or whatever makes you comfortable."

I choose to stick with the Bible on this one. "The Lord, he is God. There is none else beside him" (Deuteronomy 4:35). "There is no other God" (2 Samuel 7:22). "I am the first, and I am the last; beside me there is no God" (Isaiah 44:6). "There is but one God" (1 Timothy 2:5).

To work the Seventh Step, you must ask . . . God.

PART C: "TO REMOVE"

Many of us have asked God to help us with our shortcomings. Others have sought to better manage their shortcomings. But *remove* them? Now, that's a tall order. Let me explain what this means by the process of elimination. There are four things this does not mean.

1. **"We humbly asked God to cover our shortcomings."** This seems like a good idea on its face. And this fits what addicts have done for centuries. We try to live one life publicly while covering our secret life. That's why I jokingly say that "successful" sex addicts are the smartest people I know. Covering a secret life is not easy to pull off. But we try it, and even ask for God's help. And if he can't (or won't) cover our most heinous actions, surely we can ask him to cover our other shortcomings, right? No.

2. **"We humbly asked God to pass over our shortcomings."** The reasoning goes like this. We are basically good people. We don't deserve to be judged by our worst behaviors on our worst days. After all, many of us "only" act out a few times a week. We don't spend a lot of money on our habit, and we hide it well, so who are we really hurting? Other people get away with far more, we reason. So why not just ask God to pass over all of our shortcomings?

3. "**We humbly asked God to ignore our short-comings.**" If he won't cover our defects or pass over them, perhaps God can just ignore them. Look the other way. Let us exercise the very free wills he created us with in the first place. Besides, we are making real effort to be better people and we are trying to do the right thing. We may not be there yet, but we are on the right track.

4. "**We humbly asked God to minimize our short-comings.**" Most of us are guilty at this point. We fall into two ditches in life. We maximize or we minimize. We maximize things that aren't too important while minimizing things that are—starting with our shortcomings. It's not that they don't matter; they just don't matter that much.

Of course, none of these substitutes equals the real thing. We need our shortcomings to be removed. And we ask God to do this because we have pretty much proven we can't do this on our own.

PART D: "OUR SHORTCOMINGS"

This is where the Seventh Step ends: "*We humbly asked God to remove our shortcomings.*" This is where we admit our problem is far worse than sex addiction. As I like to say, "Sex addiction isn't a bad problem as much as it is a bad solution." If we address our sexual issues in isolation, we will miss the broader point. It is not uncommon to find dual addicts—men and women who struggle with sexually compulsive behaviors as well as problems with alcohol, drugs, tobacco, gambling, etc.

Said another way, the issue isn't the issue. There is more to it than sex. That is why we often see sex addicts come into SA or SAA meetings with a strong focus on this one issue. But they continue to drink heavily and smoke daily. It always catches up with them.

John Bunyan said, "One leak will sink a ship, and one sin will destroy a sinner."[7] But too many of us continue to leak. A major reason is that, according to a 2017 Lifeway study, only two-thirds of us even think we are sinners.[8] And those who do recognize their sin condition minimize their behaviors. I recently read an online article that identified five sins (as designated by Scripture) that most Christians pretty much ignore: gluttony, lust, pride, hate (which Jesus equated with murder), and idolatry.

We all have shortcomings. But they cannot be negotiated with; they must be eliminated. It's not enough to cover them, pass over them, ignore them, or minimize them. We must come to Christ with the same intensity that gripped the heart of the centurion on behalf of his dying servant. We must get desperate in order to get well.

Here's a good starting point. I pray the Seventh Step Prayer every day. I suggest you do the same, starting right now. If you are ready to humbly ask God to remove your shortcomings, help is on the way.

SEVENTH STEP PRAYER

"My Creator, I am now willing that you should have all of me, good and bad. I pray that you now remove from me every single defect of character which stands in the way of my usefulness to you and my fellows. Grant me strength, as I go out from here, to do your bidding."

STEP EIGHT

ZACCHAEUS

LUKE 19:1-10
*"We made a list of all persons we had harmed, and
became willing to make amends to them all."*

I preached my first revival when I was 17. The church
was small, but friendly. Though the church was in a
rural farm community, it was a growing, healthy congregation. We had several decisions for Christ that
week, and the church continued to prosper for years.

Fast forward 20 years . . .

I was driving in that same area for the first time
since preaching in that country church, so I decided
to drop by and see how the church was doing. To my
shock, the building was no longer there. It turns out
the church had closed about ten years earlier.

I wanted to know why, so I did some digging. It
turns out, the only deacons in the church—two brothers—had a falling out. Both had done and said harm-
ful things, and neither was willing to reconcile. The
church took sides, and was split down the middle. This

sapped the vision and energy from the small congregation. It wasn't long before they closed their doors.

August Wilson said, "Confront the dark parts of yourself, and work to banish them with illumination and forgiveness. Your willingness to wrestle with your demons will cause your angels to sing."[1]

Step Eight requires us to wrestle with our demons. This process can be triggering, for it takes you back to your lowest moments when you were using others to feed your addiction. Because this disease affects those around us, we have work to do—beyond our own healing. In fact, this is a part of our ultimate healing.

I can't think of a better example of making amends than Jesus' Eighth Step encounter. It's time to meet a true amends-maker. It's time to meet Zacchaeus.

MEET ZACCHAEUS

"Zacchaeus was a wee little man,
A wee little man was he.
He climbed up in a sycamore tree
For the Lord he wanted to see.
As the Savior passed him by
He looked up in the tree.
And he said, 'Zacchaeus, you come
down from there;
For I'm going to your house today.
For I'm going to your house today.'"

Anyone who hasn't heard those words has never been to Vacation Bible School. The story of Zacchaeus has captivated the imaginations of children—and adults—for centuries. We all have that image in our minds—a short fellow climbing up a tree to see Jesus, then jumping down when Jesus called his name. But there is so much more to the story. We discover the Eighth Step in his story. It's nearly impossible to miss. Let's break it down. Here's the story of this "wee little man."

WHERE DID THIS HAPPEN?

"Jesus entered Jericho and was passing through" (Luke 19:1). Jericho was located in the Jordan Valley, just west of the Jordan River, north of the Dead Sea. It remains an oasis, a paradise with palm trees and rose gardens. The city sits 800 feet below sea level and more than 3,500 feet below Jerusalem.

Jericho was a prosperous trade city on the road from Perea to Jerusalem. A considerable amount of traffic passed through. It was home to one of Rome's principal custom houses, where Zacchaeus worked.

Jericho had a rich historic heritage. It was Jericho whose walls came tumbling down before Joshua (Joshua 6). It was Jericho where we read the bizarre story of the Levite and concubine (Judges 19-21). It was Jericho that was rebuilt as a fortress for Israel under Ahab (2 Chronicles 20). And it was Jericho that welcomed Jesus that day when he met Zacchaeus.

WHO WAS ZACCHAEUS?

Zacchaeus was a tax collector, working for the kingdom of Rome. To finance their world empire, the Romans levied heavy taxes on all nations under their control. The Jews naturally opposed these taxes because they supported a secular government and its pagan gods. But they were still forced to pay. Tax collectors were among the most despised people in Israel. Jews by birth, they chose to work for Rome and were therefore considered traitors. Making matters worse, the government allowed tax collectors to extract extra resources from the Jews in order to line their own pockets. This was cruel—but legal.

Worse yet, Zacchaeus was "chief among the publicans," meaning he presided over other tax gatherers, making even more money. It is not surprising that the Scripture would say he was rich.

WHAT HE HAD DONE

It is no wonder that the people muttered when Jesus entered the tax collector's house. He had gouged the Jews for years, making himself one of the wealthiest men in Jericho. By nature of his work, Zacchaeus was both a cheater and a turncoat. But Jesus looked past all that, and the man would become Jesus' wealthiest convert.

THE EIGHTH STEP ENCOUNTER

When we see this story through the eyes of Zacchaeus, four thoughts come to mind. As he was living out this encounter in real time, I can imagine these revelations captivating his imagination.

1. **"He sees me!"** Zacchaeus wanted to see Jesus, but he was too short to see over the crowd. So he did what any man would do; he ran ahead and climbed a sycamore tree to get a better view. Just then, "When Jesus reached the spot, he looked up and said to him, 'Zacchaeus, come down'" (Luke 19:5). Imagine what raced through his mind. Zacchaeus ran ahead of the crowd. No one would have noticed his ascent into the tree, as they were focused on Jesus and his followers. Surely, Jesus was being pressed from all sides. Still, without any notice, he stopped when he reached "the spot" (Luke 19:5). Then he looked up, right at Zacchaeus. No one else saw him but Jesus. And in the moment, Jesus saw no one but Zacchaeus. "He sees me!" thought Zacchaeus.

2. **"He knows me!"** His name was the first word that crossed the lips of Christ: "Zacchaeus." They had never met. But while Zacchaeus didn't know Jesus, Jesus knew him—by name. That's the nature of Christ. He knows

every one of us. He sees the crowd, but he treasures the individual—by name.

3. **"He wants me!"** The rest of Jesus' request said it all. "Zacchaeus, come down immediately. I must stay at your house today" (Luke 19:5). It was profound that Jesus saw him, and even more incredible that he knew him. But despite all his failures and sins, the God of the universe actually wanted him.

4. **"He must have me!"** The story continues. "So he came down at once and welcomed him gladly" (Luke 19:6). The tax collector suddenly cared nothing about his reputation, his wealth, or his standing. Jesus wanted him, and that was good enough.

ZACCHAEUS MAKES AMENDS

What happened next is what made this an Eighth Step encounter. Zacchaeus became willing to make amends to all he had hurt. And then some. Catch what Zacchaeus said. "Look, Lord! Here and now I give half of my possessions to the poor, and if I have cheated anybody out of anything, I will pay back four times the amount" (Luke 19:8).

His first response was to give half of his possessions to the poor. That's what happens with real transformation. We do things we aren't even asked to do. When a sex addict has been discovered by his spouse, that is the sign that he is serious about making things right. He doesn't do the least work possible to keep the marriage together; he does more than is asked of him.

Now it was time for more amends. Notice, Zacchaeus had not yet actually made amends (Step 9); he is planning them. The original text gives us one Greek word to describe what would come next: *sycophanted*. It is loosely translated, "If I have *taken anything by false accusation*." What he was saying was, "I can't remember all the people I've ripped off, but I want to make things right with as many of them as possible."

Why "four-fold"? Remember, Zacchaeus was a Jew. He was likely familiar with Jewish law and tradition. The Jewish law required repaying four times the amount when a sheep had been stolen and the thief was convicted by trial (Exodus 22:1). If he confessed to the crime without being detected, he would restore what was taken and add a fifth (Numbers 5:6-7).

THREE QUICK LESSONS

Luke 19 provides a prototype for addiction recovery. It's all there—desperation, surrender, disclosure, and community. Frankly, we could have used this story as an example of any of the 12 steps. Zacchaeus was a walking, breathing example of how a man acts when he finds recovery, and how his life changes as a result. Let's wrap up our discussion of Zacchaeus with three quick recovery lessons.

1. **No one is too bad to be saved or too good to be lost**. If this conniving, cheating, turncoat was within the reach of grace, so are you. If Zacchaeus had not gone too far, neither have you. And on the other extreme, remember our discussion of Nicodemus? Here we find a man who lived the ideal pious life. But he also needed salvation. Zacchaeus was not too bad to be saved and Nicodemus was not too good to be lost. I know a man who has committed every sexual sin imaginable— with women, men, children, and farm animals. As appalling as that is, he has found recovery. And I know a man who has "only" done a little pornography. But he remains in the depths of his addiction.

2. **You don't reach an addict by telling him how bad he is, but by telling him how good he can become**. Notice, Jesus did not say, "Zacchaeus, you're a horrible human being, a cheat, and a disgrace to the Jewish race." Instead, Jesus said, "Come on down. Let's hang out for a while." Jesus did not diminish or minimize his sin; he dealt with it effectively. That's how we have to be with those coming into recovery. We must proclaim grace and hope; they can always find judgment someplace else.

3. **The window for recovery will not stay open forever**. This was the first time Zacchaeus

saw Jesus. But it was also the last time Jesus would ever pass through his town of Jericho. He didn't know it at the time, but this would be his only shot at spending time with Jesus. We must preach urgency to people who are mired in their sin. No one ever got well by waiting for the next day.

THE TWO PARTS OF STEP EIGHT

God's work in your life is not complete until you make things right with others. I heard someone describe Step 8 like this: "Step Eight is where the vertical goes horizontal." They meant that recovery begins by working on our relationship with God, but it doesn't end there. We *find* recovery in God, but we *secure* recovery by the way we then treat others. Said another way, Step 4 begins the process of cleaning house, whereas Step 8 begins the process of taking out the trash.

In our active addiction, our actions and intentions are not aligned. It's fun to watch that change during recovery, as our actions begin to line up with our intentions for the first time. We begin to express grace toward others. Rick Warren says it like this: "When you have experienced grace and you feel like you've been forgiven, you are a lot more forgiving of others."[2] This sets up Step Eight perfectly. While Jesus seemed to sneak up on Zacchaeus, Zacchaeus didn't sneak up on Jesus. One commentary made this observation.

Long before Zacchaeus even thought about seeing Jesus, God had planted the tree he would need on the day for which he was born.

Here are the two parts of the Eighth Step.

MAKE A LIST.

Step Eight says we are to "make a list of all persons we have harmed." We read in *The Twelve Steps and Twelve Traditions*, "Every addict has found that he can make little headway in this new adventure of living until he first backtracks and really makes an accurate and unsparing survey of the human wreckage he has left in the wake" (p. 77).

This is a long and difficult task. Notice, while Zacchaeus seemed to breeze right through this, he only said that he would make amends to those lives he had wrecked; he didn't begin to name them all. Not yet. This takes time and prayer.

Who belongs on this list? First, the addict's name. He needs to make amends to himself. And God should be on the list. After that, family, close friends, anyone he has stolen from to feed his addiction (time or money), and acting out partners—they all need to be on his list.

It is far better to work the Eighth Step too slowly than too fast. This Step must be done thoroughly or not at all. Harriet Beecher Stowe said, "The most bitter tears shed over graves are for words left unsaid, and deeds left undone."[3] Don't let that be you. Decide today that there will be no words left unsaid and no deeds left undone.

Make a list. Check it twice. Then check it again.

BE WILLING TO MAKE AMENDS.

It's not time to make amends yet. This is the willingness phase. But this may be even harder than making the actual amends (Step Nine), because in this Step, we consider people from our past—men and women we know we will never actually contact. But we must be *willing* to contact them. Though this is not for the weak of heart, it can be done. Joan of Arc could have been speaking for every addict when she said, "I am not afraid. I was born to do this."

Let me encourage you if you are preparing your Eighth Step. When it looks like it is just too much, it's not. When the pain seems too great, it's not. When you feel like you can't continue, you can. I have observed hundreds of men and women who have found successful recovery. And I have seen too many who have failed. In most cases, this is what I have found. The reason we tend to give up is that we look at how far we have to go instead of how far we have already come.

You have come too far to quit now. It's time to make that list. It's time to embrace a willingness to make amends to all you have hurt. It's time to work the Eighth Step.

STEP NINE

THE WEEPING APOSTLE

MATTHEW 26:31-35, 69-75
"We made direct amends to such people wherever possible, except when to do so would injure them or others."

A Christian man was faced with a real life Ninth Step challenge. He was a boat builder who used copper nails in his work. While building huge ships for his boss, the man was also building a small boat at home for his own use. But he couldn't afford copper nails for his personal work. The temptation was great, so he caved one day. He took a handful of copper nails from work home with him to use on his own boat. This escalated, until he had stolen enough copper nails to complete his personal project.

But the Holy Spirit would not let him rest. As in an audible voice, God was saying, "Repay your boss and tell him what you have done."

The man had a sincere problem with this. For years, he had been sharing his faith with the wealthy man. If he confessed stealing the copper nails, the boss would see him as a hypocrite, and his witness for Christ would be blown.

He couldn't sleep at night, so he finally gave in. One morning, he walked into his boss' office and unloaded it all. He confessed everything.

"Why didn't you tell me this earlier?" asked his boss.

"Well, it's really pretty simple," the man said. "As you know, I'm a Christian, and I want you to know my God. But I was afraid that if you saw me as a hypocrite, you would never consider following Christ."

"To the contrary," replied the man's boss. "I figure that any religion that would make a dishonest worker come back and confess that he had been stealing a few copper nails must be worth having."

The Ninth Step—the one that makes amends—it neither easy nor optional. It is the step that actor Jason Wahler calls the "biggie step." The book, *The Steps We Took*, says this: "If we don't do Steps Eight and Nine, our defects will continue to dominate our minds and block us off from God."[1] The Scripture tells us that we must "make full restitution for the wrong we have done" (Numbers 5:7).

BEFORE WE GET TO PETER

We will introduce a real-life Ninth-stepper in a bit. (Until then, ignore the subtitle above so you will be surprised to read who it is.) The fact is, the Bible is actually full of Ninth Step men and women. Having completed the first seven steps, their recovery turned from vertical (connecting with God) to horizontal (connecting with others). First, they "made a list of all persons they had harmed, and became willing to make amends to them all" (Step Eight). Step Nine moves us from willingness to action. We will take a quick survey of a few characters who took the plunge, who "made direct amends to such people wherever possible, except when to do so would injure them or others" (Step Nine).

STEP-NINER #1: MEPHIBOSHETH

Here's his story. (Try to keep up!) King Saul was David's nemesis. At every turn, he tried to have the lad killed. A special bond was forged between Jonathan, Saul's son, and David. Jonathan protected his good friend from his father many times. In return, David pledged his undying support for Jonathan. He committed to blessing Jonathan and his family.

Sadly, both Saul and Jonathan died in battle, against the Philistines. At the time, Jonathan had a young five-year-old son named Mephibosheth. After the deaths of his father and grandfather, Mephibosheth's nurse took him and fled in panic. In her haste, she dropped the boy, causing a lifetime injury. The boy would never be able to walk again.

Fast forward several years. Young David had become King David. He remembered his pledge to Solomon, to whom he owed his very life. But Solomon was no longer available to receive the new king's blessing. Therefore, David sought out someone from Jonathan's lineage to bless. When they brought Mephibosheth to him, he restored Saul's inheritance to him and welcomed him into his palace. In his own words, "I will restore to you all the land that belonged to your grandfather Saul, and you will always eat at my table" (2 Samuel 9:7).

STEP-NINER #2: ZACCHAEUS

We studied the "wee little man" in chapter 8, so I'll be brief here. Having stolen from common tax payers, Zacchaeus became a changed man, which led to changed behavior. He committed to pay those he had harmed four times over, as required by Jewish law (Exodus 22).

Sometimes, we only get one shot to take the Ninth Step. Zacchaeus was an example of that. He only met Jesus one time, as far as we can tell. If he had put off the Ninth Step, the moment would have soon passed. This step doesn't require endless planning and calculations. It requires action, action, and more action. To that end, Zacchaeus knocked it out of the park.

STEP-NINER #3: PAUL

When Paul was dramatically transformed on the Damascus Road, he made an astonishing turnaround. Having been a persecutor of Christians, he was soon ready to live a lifetime of amends. Paul would not only live for Christ; he would eventually die for Him.

So astounding was his life change that others observed, "Is not this the man who made havoc in Jerusalem for those who called upon this name [of Jesus]?" (Acts 9:21).

It's not that hard to fake Christianity. You can learn the jargon pretty quickly. At least I did. You can learn to talk right and walk right. At least I did. You can learn when to "Amen" at church and how to call everyone "brother." At least I did.

My old pastor, Dr. Cecil Sewell, says it like this: "You can give without loving, but you can't love without giving." In other words, you can fake Christianity— but only to a point.

In making amends, we move into radical territory. Let me propose the irony of ironies. I suggest that it is one thing to bless those who have hurt us. But it actually takes more to bless those whom we have hurt. And that is why so few ever conquer the Ninth Step. But the one in whose strength "all things are possible" can make it happen.

Dr. Craig Cashwell said it well: In *Shadows of the Cross*, Cashwell writes, "Making amends is a difficult and painful process, but it also liberates you from the guilt of past behaviors so that you can live more fully in the relationship you have with Christ."[2]

THE WEEPING APOSTLE

Before Peter gave his life for Christ, crucified upside down, he was the man who wrote two letters that became Scripture. Before he was that man, he was the man of whom Jesus said, "I will build my church." Before he was that man, he preached the great sermon of Pentecost. Before he was that man, he celebrated the resurrected Christ. And before he was that man, he denied Jesus three times.

You would be hard pressed to find anyone in the Bible with more issues than Peter. He was insecure, a braggart, loud, and self-absorbed. Peter was often wrong but never in doubt. He was the perfect candidate to relapse into his old ways on the eve of the crucifixion. But what made Peter special was that no matter how many slips and relapses he had, he always got up.

It's what Peter did after he fell that matters. We will see this as Peter's life unfolds in three parts, all recorded in Matthew 26.

ACT I—WHAT PETER DID FIRST

"Then Jesus told them, 'This very night you will all fall away on account of me, for it is written: I will strike the shepherd, and the sheep of the flock will be scattered. But after I have risen, I will go ahead of you into Galilee.' Peter replied, 'Even if all fall away on account of you, I never will.' 'Truly I tell you,' Jesus answered, 'This very night, before the rooster crows, you will disown me three

times.' But Peter declared, 'Even if I have to die with you, I will never disown you.' And all the other disciples said the same" (Matthew 26:31-35).

In Peter's bold declaration, I find three valuable recovery lessons.

1. **We all fall**. Notice what Jesus predicted: "This very night you will *all* fall away" (Matthew 26:31). We focus on Peter, but he wasn't the only one who fell. We are all fallen creatures. We all have issues. It's the human condition.
2. **Never say you'll never fail**. I hear it a lot. Men get into recovery and are really fired up about their future. After decades of failure, they experience real hope. In their enthusiasm they promise their wives, "I will never act out again." We are like Peter, who boldly declared, "Even if all fall away on account of you, I never will" (Matthew 26:33). Peter kept his word right up until a few minutes later. My promise to my wife today is this: "I don't promise that I'll never act out again. But I do promise it won't happen today." For me, that works. Recovery is a daily thing, not an annual thing. My sobriety tomorrow is dependent on what I do today. But then I have to work my program of recovery again the next day, and the next—for the rest of my life.

3. **Don't overpromise**. Peter said, "Even if I have to die with you, I will never disown you" (Matthew 26:35). Deal with the temptations of today. Pride comes before fall. You have enough struggles in the life you are really living without venturing into the unknown.

ACT II—WHAT PETER DID WRONG

"Now Peter was sitting out in the courtyard, and a servant girl came to him. 'You also were with Jesus of Galilee,' she said. But he denied it before them all. 'I don't know what you're talking about,' he said. Then he went out to the gateway, where another servant girl saw him and said to the people there, 'This fellow was with Jesus of Nazareth.' He denied it again, with an oath: 'I don't know the man!' After a little while, those standing there went up to Peter and said, 'Surely you are one of them; your accent gives you away.' Then he began to call down curses, and he swore to them, 'I don't know the man!' Immediately a rooster crowed" (Matthew 26:69-75).

Peter was quick to deny he'd ever deny. His oath was direct: "It'll never happen—period." And then it did. Let's take a look at what went wrong.

1. **Peter was alone**. He was found sitting in the courtyard alone, apart from the other disciples. He was a sitting duck, as "a servant girl came to him" (Matthew 26:69). Most addic-

tion is rooted in one of three things: abuse, trauma, or isolation. Peter was isolated.

2. **Peter was defensive**. "I don't know what you're talking about," he shouted (Matthew 26:70). Every addict struggles with defensiveness. We deny and deflect. It's what we do best.

3. **Peter's denial escalated**. First, Peter denied knowing Jesus. Then he denied him with an oath, which is a legal term. Finally, he "began to call down curses, and he swore to them, 'I don't know the man!'" (Matthew 27:72-74). Peter's denial escalated from diversion to insistence to curses.

ACT III—WHAT PETER DID RIGHT

"Immediately a rooster crowed. Then Peter remembered the word Jesus had spoken: 'Before the rooster crows, you will disown me three times.' And he went outside and wept bitterly" (Matthew 26:75).

It's easy to pile on. We judge others by their actions, while judging ourselves by our intentions. Enter Peter. Let's be honest—he blew it. The man denied even knowing his Savior three times, to an unintimidating servant girl. But God wasn't done with him, not by a long shot. We see redemption in the final two words of the chapter. Peter *wept bitterly*.

1. **Peter remembered**. He had not strayed so far from his Savior that he could no longer recognize the message of the rooster. He remembered Jesus' words. He remembered his own promises. He remembered a thing called grace.

2. **Peter wept bitterly**. The second thing Peter did right was unbecoming to a man of his culture. He broke down emotionally. The word for "bitterly" is *pikros*. It comes from the word that refers to being pierced with a sword. The sound of the rooster's crow reminded him of the sound of the Savior's voice. And that brought tears to his eyes and brokenness to his heart.

We've seen (a) what Peter did first, (b) what Peter did wrong, and (c) what Peter did right. We are all Peters. Let's make it personal. *We are all like Peter.* Sexual brokenness and addictive behaviors have driven you from the right path and the true God. But it's what comes next that matters. When you come face to face with your failures, how do you respond? Peter did it right. Peter wept bitterly.

THREE KINDS OF AMENDS

In *Healing the Wounds of Sexual Addiction*, Mark Laaser tells the story of a wealthy client who had spent over $3 million on his addiction. The man confessed, "All that sex was never enough. I always wanted more."[3] I like to say it this way—addiction will take you further than you want to go, it will keep you longer than you want to stay, and it will cost you more than you want to pay.

One of the exits from the crazy train is Step Nine—making amends. We have seen several examples from Scripture. But not all amends are created equal. There are actually three distinct types of amends to be made: direct, indirect, and living. In summary, Tim Stoddart, of Sober Nation, breaks down these three: "Direct amends deal with taking personal responsibility and confronting the person with whom you want to reconcile. Indirect amends are ways to repair damage that cannot be physically undone. A living amend is a positive way to display to others and to prove to yourself that you have evolved from the person that you used to be. Living amends is a promise to yourself that you have made a genuine lifestyle change. This is a marked end to the destructive patterns that you have been living with and a beacon for change and prosperity."[4]

DIRECT AMENDS

We read in the *Twelve Steps and Twelve Traditions*, "We made direct amends to such people wherever possible, except when to do so would injure them or others."[5] Direct amends demand a readiness to own the consequences of our acts. The Dream Center for

Recovery says, "Step Nine can be seen as a make or break step because not only are you sincerely apologizing to those you have hurt because of your actions, but you also need to prove with your actions that you are committed to your recovery." Let's consider four questions about direct amends.

1. **What is the purpose of working the Ninth Step**? When you make amends, it is not for others, but to secure your own recovery. The success of making amends is found in your obedience, not the response of someone else. Dr. Tamar Chansky, author of *Freeing Yourself from Anxiety,* writes, "You don't do it to get a particular outcome, but to do the right thing from your side and clear your conscience."[6]

2. **To whom are direct amends made**? When possible, amends should be made in person. We read in the AA Big Book, "The only exceptions we will make will be cases where our disclosure would cause actual harm."[7] While it is true that we make amends as a part of our recovery, we often find that this process is a huge blessing to the other party. Dr. Michael McCullough, professor of psychology at the University of Miami, says, "All of the things that people are motivated to do when they have harmed someone they care

about really do appear to be effective at helping victims forgive and get over their anger."[8]

3. **When do we make direct amends**? Generally, this should come within the natural flow
of working the 12 Steps. Step Nine is *Step
Nine* for a reason. We are not ready to make
amends early in our recovery. There is a process to be followed. However, this is the step
we must work a little every day. If your addiction has devastated your wife, for example,
you can't tell her, "I'd love to tell you more
about what I have done and begin the work
of reconciliation, but I need to work Steps
One-Eight first."

4. **How do we make direct amends**? I always
suggest writing them out, then reviewing
them with one's sponsor, before moving forward. Then it is wise to read the amends, to
be sure we say what is intended and necessary.

INDIRECT AMENDS

It is not always wise to make direct amends. But
it is always necessary to make amends. That is where
indirect amends come in. We make direct amends by
repairing the damage we have done. We make indirect
amends by repairing the attitudes that caused us to
do damage in the first place, helping to ensure that we
won't cause further damage in the future. The process

of determining which amends are to be direct vs. indirect cannot be taken lightly.

Start with your Eighth Step list of people to whom you owe amends. Narrow the list to those you can approach directly. In cases in which amends might injure the other person (or any person, for that matter), we move to indirect amends.

Indirect amends often consist of two things. First, write out your amends to each person, then present each letter to your sponsor for review. Second, look for substitute opportunities to make amends. For example, if you have spent money on prostitutes, rather than going to these women in person (direct amends), write a check to a sex trafficking agency. Rather than going to your boss and admitting to stealing money to indulge your addiction, make a gift to charity.

LIVING AMENDS

This is the fun part. Unlike direct and indirect amends, living amends are done for a lifetime. Dr. Jennifer Matesa, author of *The Recovering Body*, says, "The best way to make amends isn't just to apologize, but to change the hurtful behavior."[9] In short, to make living amends means to live a life of sobriety and recovery. While living amends do not require making a list or arranging a meeting, they are the most important amends. While this never requires direct confrontation or dialogue, living amends are among the purest examples of a life truly committed to recovery.

In making direct amends, you sit down with a person you have harmed, read them your letter, then leave the results in God's hands. In making indirect amends, you read the letter to your sponsor, then move on. But in making living amends, you demonstrate a life of contrition and sober living.

STEP TEN

BUILDING A TOWER

LUKE 14:25-33

"We continued to take personal inventory, and when we were wrong, we promptly admitted it."

An old man, a boy, and a donkey were walking to town. The boy rode on the donkey and the old man walked. As they went along the road, they passed some critics who remarked that it was a shame that the old man was walking while the boy got to ride the donkey. The man and boy agreed that the critics were probably right, so they changed positions. Later, they passed some more people who remarked, "What a shame, that grown man makes the little boy walk." So they decided they both would walk.

Soon they passed another group of onlookers, who thought they were stupid to walk when they had a perfectly good donkey on which to ride. So, they both rode the donkey. Then they passed another group who commented on how awful it was to put such a load on the poor donkey. Thus, the man and the boy agreed that these people must be right, and they decided to carry the donkey.

Nearing a river, the man and the boy approached a bridge, carrying their donkey. As they crossed over, they lost their grip on the donkey and he fell into the river and drowned.

Jennifer Porter, a contributor to the *Harvard Business Review*, states, "The most useful reflection involves the conscious consideration and analysis of beliefs and actions for the purpose of learning."[1]

The old man and the boy were wise to listen to what others had to say. They were practicing the Tenth Step. As they heard the critics, they took personal inventory. But they didn't do it correctly. Let me be clear—*working the Tenth Step incorrectly is worse than not working it at all.*

Our Tenth Step story of Jesus involves a dual parable.

PARABLE #1—THE TOWER

"Suppose one of you wants to build a tower. Won't you first sit down and estimate the cost to see if you have enough money to complete it? For if you lay the foundation and are not able to finish it, everyone who sees it will ridicule you, saying, 'This person began to build and wasn't able to finish'" (Luke 14:28-30).

When Jesus offered a parable, it was always a vivid image with which his immediate audience could connect. In this case, the "tower" he had in mind was likely a vineyard tower. Vineyards were often equipped with towers from which watch was kept against thieves who might steal the harvest. If left unfinished, the tower became a laughingstock to the man's neighbors.

An unfinished tower was actually worse than not building any tower at all. When left unfinished, the message was, "We are not ready to defend our vineyard." An incomplete tower would cast a shadow of doubt and defeat over the vineyard. It represented weakness, half-hearted commitment, and a people who could easily be defeated. All they had spent years planting could be stolen in a moment. While the vineyard may have been productive, there was no defense to keep the enemy out.

Step Ten says we do two things: continue to take personal inventory and make corrections as needed. The incomplete tower is the picture of the addict who stops his recovery work just short of Step Ten. He has built nine steps of solid recovery, including the most difficult Steps Four and Nine. But his failure to continue to take personal inventory and make corrections as needed has left him vulnerable to attack from the outside.

PARABLE #2—THE KING'S ARMY

"Or suppose a king is about to go to war against another king. Won't he first sit down and consider whether

*he is able with ten thousand men to oppose the one com-
ing against him with twenty thousand? If he is not able, he
will send a delegation while the other is still a long way off
and will ask for terms of peace"* (Luke 14:31-32).

In 1848 Charles Raine designed a house that
would make history. Raine sold his house in Appomat-
tox, Virginia, to a man named Wilmer McLean in 1863.
It was at that house that the most famous surrender
that ever took place on American soil occurred just
two years later.

In fierce fighting, Gen. Robert E. Lee lost 500
men to the Union Army of Northern Virginia in the
Spring of 1865. His remaining force of 27,805 men
was starving and badly outnumbered by Gen. Ulysses
S. Grant's army of 150,000 men. Lee took inventory of
the situation. His army was cornered and had no hope
of victory. He had only two options: surrender or die.
He loved his men too much to continue fighting.

On April 9, 1865, Robert E. Lee did the noble
thing. He surrendered his army to Gen. Grant, effectively ending the Civil War. What he really did was a
form of the Tenth Step. Though he had continued to
fight against all odds, he took a personal inventory of
the situation, and realized his current strategy was
wrong, and before Ulysses S. Grant and his own men,
he promptly admitted it.

In Jesus' second example of the Tenth Step, he
again speaks the language of the common people.

This is how war was conducted—a king went to war against another king. In fact, the king traditionally led the men into battle. You may recall that King David remained home at the palace—and got into trouble because of it—"at the time when kings march off to war" (2 Samuel 11:1).

The first thing a king did was to take a careful inventory of the size and condition of his army, as well as the armor and weapons they had on hand. In those days of hand-to-hand combat, the advantage basically came down to simple numbers. The army with the most men won.

INVENTORY—WHAT'S THE BIG DEAL?

Minnesota Senator Amy Klobuchar said, "As an intern for Vice President Walter Mondale, I arrived the first day ready to write policy memos and change the world. But my assignment was to do an inventory of the furniture."[2]

Introspection and personal inventory transcend the 12 Steps and even biblical teaching. Before Alcoholics Anonymous was created (1939) people were taking inventory. Before Robert E. Lee was appointed to lead the Southern troops, military leaders took inventory.

There are several reasons we take personal inventories.

1. **Taking inventory is a part of personal growth**. Thomas Paine said, "The real man smiles in trouble, gathers strength from distress, and grows brave by reflection." We cannot grow in our recovery, relationships, or spiritual lives until we complete an accurate assessment of where we live in the present.

2. **Inventories connect us with others**. This is why it is always recommended to work the 12 Steps with the assistance of a sponsor and within the context of a group. The input of others is critical to our inventories. John F. Kennedy said it like this: "To state the facts frankly is not to despair the future nor indict the past. The prudent heir takes careful inventory of his legacies and gives a faithful accounting to those whom he owes an obligation of trust."

3. **Inventories catapult us into action**. Max Dupree famously said, "The first task of a leader is to define reality as it is." Naomi Wolf said, "Every Yom Kippur, Jewish tradition requires a strict spiritual inventory. You aren't supposed to just sit around feeling guilty, but to take action in the real world to set things right."

4. **Inventories feed recovery**. Every day, you will either feed your addiction or you will feed your recovery. Milton Magness and

Marsha Means write, in *Real Hope, True Freedom*, "As recovery progresses, cravings and urges to act out lessen in both frequency and intensity. That being said, most sex addicts with long-term sobriety will report they have occasional thoughts of acting out. One of the gifts of recovery is learning to recognize the thoughts, emotions, and experiences that trigger cravings and then use the tools of recovery to counteract them. Since you are a sexual being, you will have sexual thoughts throughout your life. Recovery will help you make peace with your sexual thoughts so you can live in co-existence with them instead of returning to the chaos of addiction."[3]

THE Q.U.I.C.K. METHOD

How do we take a personal inventory? Within the context of 12-Step work, one's sponsor is usually equipped to walk the newcomer through this process. There are several tools available that help. The fact is, there is no perfect way to work the Tenth Step—or any other step, for that matter. The main thing is not how we work it, but that we work it. Joyce Meyer said, "Instead of blaming everyone and everything else for your problems, pray for God to help you take an inventory of what's been on your mind so you can think about what you've been thinking about."

The business world is replete with direction in this arena. Harry Kraemer, former CEO of Baxter International, stated, "Instead of constant acceleration, leadership demands periods of restraint and consideration."[4] JM Olejarz, in *Harvard Business Review*, suggests three simple components of any inventory: (a) start with a few important questions, (b) schedule times to review your inventory, and (c) start small (November 2015).[5]

I like the formula offered by Dr. A. Douglass Eury, professor at Gardner-Webb University. Dr. Eury has developed a simple five-part template that facilitates a "Q.U.I.C.K." personal inventory:[6]

Q = Question yourself. Ask yourself how you are doing—in recovery, in this case. Make this a frequent activity.

U = Understand how to get to your objective. Make plans. Start with where you are, but don't stay there. Plan a process to meet the goals you have set for yourself.

I = Inquire of others. There is wisdom in many counselors. Take advantage of the men and women God has put in your life. Ask for opinions. Lean on others.

C = Complete honesty. Whether building a tower, measuring an army, or working recovery, it is important to be painfully honest in one's assessment.

K = Keep a journal. Write down your thoughts, assessments, and goals. We remember only a fraction of what we hear, as opposed to what we write.

WHAT TO INCLUDE

If you took a spaceship to the moon, but miscalculated your direction by just 0.5 percent, you'd miss the moon by 200,000 miles. Taking a thorough and accurate inventory is critical to getting where you need to be, in space travel and in recovery. The problem is we all want the inventory, but we don't want to do the work to get it done. Like Step Four, the process must be both thorough and fearless.

When I was a boy, my Dad owned his own business. He was an electronics components sales rep. That meant he sold electronics parts on behalf of huge factories, to oil companies, mostly located in Texas. His time was largely dedicated to calling on old customers, potential customers, and visiting the six factories, which he represented around the country. But Dad also sold small orders on the side.

Dad ordered capacitors and reel relays directly from the factory. He stored them in boxes in a designated room at his office. Then, when companies needed a small order filled, he'd ship the parts directly, which expedited the process. It was smart business.

My brother and I liked to hang out at the office during the summer, so Dad decided to put us to work. He paid us to count inventory. We got paid one dollar for every box we counted. Some boxes had as many as 40-50 parts, while others had just one. Jim and I would just randomly select boxes, count the parts, then write the number of parts on a small sheet of paper and put that paper in the box.

One day, while my brother earned about $5, I made over $20. Here's how. I only counted the boxes with one or two parts in them. If I came upon a box with dozens of tiny parts, I slid that box back into its place. Every box paid $1, so why waste my time on the boxes with so many parts?

A lot of us do our personal inventory the way I did Dad's inventory. When we slide out a box and find a lot of stuff in there, we slide it back in. We only do real inventory on the easy stuff.

In our stories from Luke 14, we saw that easy inventory is no inventory. The owner of the vineyard had to complete his inventory of the tower and the king had to complete his inventory of his army. They had to see if they had what they needed to complete the job. The same is true in recovery. You need to take a very specific inventory, to see if you have what it takes to complete the job.

The following is certainly not a complete inventory list, but it's a good start. A good, honest, Tenth Step inventory should answer these questions.

1. How is my relationship with God?
2. Am I sober today?
3. Would those closest to me say I'm sober?
4. What am I doing to secure my sobriety tomorrow?
5. Am I attending groups?
6. Am I helping others?
7. Am I living inside my head?
8. How is my fantasy life doing?
9. Am I sliding into my middle circle behaviors?
10. Do I have personal accountability?
11. How am I doing with my character defects?
12. Have I added tools to my recovery toolbox this year?
13. Am I living in complete surrender?

BRINGING IT HOME

In *Rethinking Sexuality*, Dr. Juli Slattery wrote, "What you think about sex begins with what you believe about God."[7] The Tenth Step inventory begins with your relationship with God. You can't build the tower and win the war without Him. You can't maintain sobriety, let alone recovery without Him. You can't live in sanity and freedom without Him.

No matter how far you have traveled down the road to recovery, the ditch on the side of the road is still just as close. In my adolescent years, when we traveled as a family, I was the designated navigator. Why? Because I was good at reading the old Rand Mc-Nally maps. My job was to make sure we were headed in the right direction. And if we got off the main road, my job was to do a quick inventory by finding the road back to the highway.

We all get off the highway from time to time. Some wander further than others. And that's okay. What's not okay is driving into the ditch, or so far down some secondary road that you are no longer going in the right direction. One man in the Gospel account was trying to build something special. The other man was trying to win the war. In recovery, you are doing both. As you build the life God has for you and win the battles every day, you need the map. You must take inventory. And when you find that you are wrong—and you will be sometimes—promptly admit it.

STEP ELEVEN

THE WALK TO EMMAUS

LUKE 24:13-53

"We sought through prayer and meditation to improve our conscious contact with God as we understood him, praying only for knowledge of his will for us and the power to carry it out."

Bill W., the founder of Alcoholics Anonymous, wasn't always a believer in God. Before writing the Big Book, Bill had been a skeptic about all things spiritual. In his autobiography, he described himself as "incapable of faith." That would change, as Bill came to see himself as an alcoholic doomed to an early death unless he stopped drinking.

One night, during a hospital stay, Bill cried out, "If there be a God, let him show himself." We read, in *Bill W.: My First 40 Years*, "Suddenly, my room blazed with an indescribable white light. I was seized with an ecstasy beyond description. Then came the blazing thought, 'You are a free man.'"[1]

After that night, Bill never drank again. The story of his "white light" experience became a mainstay of AA tradition. Eventually, Bill visited a psychiatrist and came away with a notion of sanity—rooted in a spiritual connection.

As he grew in his faith, Bill was influenced by the Oxford Group, a movement dedicated to rediscovering the principles of early Christianity. He embraced a daily practice of prayer and meditation, which he called his "quiet time."

Step Eleven came to life. Bill learned that recovery—lasting recovery—is dependent on prayer and meditation as the vehicles to an improved conscious contact with God.

St. Augustine said, "To fall in love with God is the greatest romance; to seek him the greatest adventure; to find him, the greatest human achievement."[2] This is the essence of the Eleventh Step. Developing our "conscious contact with God" is not only at the center of Step Eleven; it is foundational for lasting recovery.

Let's consider an Eleventh Step story for the ages.

THE LONG WALK HOME

Let's set the stage. The city was Jerusalem. The event was Passover. The day was resurrection Sunday. The two men were Cleopas and his friend. Their home was Emmaus, seven miles to the west.

The two men—their identity is largely speculative—were in Jerusalem for the religious event of the year. Jesus had just been raised from the dead. These men got word that the body of Jesus was missing. While they knew his teachings and predictions of a resurrection, they lived in their worst fears. That Jesus could actually fulfill his promises was beyond their comprehension.

The two men set out on the long walk home. For the next three hours they would reminisce about the good old days when Jesus still walked among them. As "they discussed everything that had happened" (Luke 24:15), Jesus joined them on the road, soon engaging in their discussion. Not recognizing that it was Jesus, they told him their account of the events of the past three days.

Jesus reminded them of his teachings and the prophesy of the resurrection. But their eyes were not opened until they invited Jesus to stay with them and he broke bread with them. Their response was immediate. "They got up and returned at once to Jerusalem" to tell the disciples the good news (Luke 24:33).

There is more to unpack from this story than fits our purpose here. Our focus is on the application of Jesus' personal teachings and experiences on the 12 Steps. We will limit our discussion to the lessons from the passage that apply to the Steps. I see nine pertinent lessons.

LESSON 1: PAIN IS ROOTED IN TRAUMA AND ISOLATION.

Dr. Gabor Mate said in a 2017 interview, "Whether we are talking about the emotional pain and the shame that's at the heart of addiction or whether we are looking at the brain physiology of addiction, we are looking at the impact of trauma."[3] Dr. Frank McAndrew adds, "Isolation can lead to a profoundly altered state of consciousness."[4]

The men in our story suffered from both trauma and isolation. They were traumatized by disappointment, convinced that Jesus—to whom they had committed their lives—would usher in the long-awaited Jewish kingdom. Then Jesus was crucified, and they completely shut down. The trauma was so deep that they couldn't even conceive of the possibility that Jesus' death might fulfill God's plan rather than derail it.

An anonymous writer said it like this: "My past is an armor I cannot take off, no matter how many times you tell me the war is over." In these two men we find the depths of trauma and isolation, just as they are at the heart of every addiction.

1. **Trauma**: We find one of the saddest verses in Scripture within this passage. "We had hoped that he was the one who was going to redeem Israel" (Luke 24:21). Don't miss those three horrifying words: *"We had hoped."* It is no wonder that their faces were "downcast"

(Luke 24:17). They had lost all hope. Hope is the one thing that keeps us going when all else fails. Hope gets the paraplegic back to the rehab facility and the broken couple back to the therapist. Hope is what enables the addict to pray and his wife to stay. The door through which hope exits is the door through which trauma enters the room. The process is as predictable as it is sad: hope leaves, trauma enters, addiction follows.

2. **Isolation**: "Two of them were going to a village called Emmaus" (Luke 24:13). These two men were walking in the wrong direction at the wrong time in the wrong crowd. First, they were walking in the wrong direction—away from Jerusalem. As they walked west toward Emmaus, with every step they got further away from the birthplace of the church, where groups would soon spring up to spread the Good News. Second, they were walking at the wrong time. The depth of their trauma was the precise time they needed to be in Jerusalem. Third, these two men chose the wrong crowd—each other! They needed the warm embrace of the apostles and other intimate followers of Christ. Instead, they withdrew to an isolation that would plunge them deeper into depression.

LESSON 2: GOD IS CLOSER THAN YOU THINK.

"As they talked and discussed these things with each other, Jesus himself came up and walked with them, but they were kept from recognizing him" (Luke 24:15-16). Man's inability to see God or to recognize him does not invalidate his presence. You can *experience* God's presence without *feeling* God's presence.

I was 19 years old when Dad died. His death was as painful as it was sudden. The next three days were a blur, as we planned the funeral service, notified his business associates, and put legal documents and finances in order. But I remember the service well—the sermon by my pastor, the music, and the eulogies. I remember many who were in the chapel—my mom, brother, other family, close friends, church members, and neighbors. But to be honest, the last person I knew was in the room was God.

I felt alone and abandoned. But mostly, I was scared. Dad was always there for me. The last time I saw him was seven days before he died, when he installed a power steering unit in my car (which he had paid for). But I slowly learned that, while Dad had gone away, my Father hadn't gone anywhere. In fact, he was closer than I could have imagined.

Whether you have felt the pain of abandonment, trauma, or a cousin of either, make Jen Jolly's words your own. In her time of loss, she shouted to anyone close enough to hear, "Don't give up on me when I isolate!" The really good news is, God is closer than you think.

LESSON 3: YOU CAN EXPERIENCE GOD'S PRESENCE WITHOUT FEELING IT.

Notice the odd progression: (a) the men walked alone, (b) Jesus joined them, and (c) "they stood still, their faces downcast" (Luke 24:17). Jesus was right there with them, but they didn't know it. God's presence was very real, but they didn't feel it. In recovery, it is important to put right actions ahead of right feelings. There is an old saying in 12-Step meetings that goes like this: "Just bring the body." In other words, if we will do the work, regardless of the feelings, recovery will come.

I am often frustrated by chronic slips by some who claim to be in recovery. They identify all kinds of excuses. But every acting out event is a choice. We make choices all day that fly in the face of the feelings of the moment. The same should be true in recovery. The key is to work the program regardless of how we feel. And we must trust God's presence, whether we feel it or not.

LESSON 4: THE ANSWER IS NOT MORE INFORMATION.

Cleopas and his friend had plenty of knowledge. They talked about it for hours, discussing everything that had happened (Luke 24:14). When Jesus joined their walk, they told him all about the events of the past few days (Luke 24:19-24). Still, when Jesus explained the resurrection to them, they were not convinced (Luke 24:25-27).

The difference maker came a bit later. "When he was at the table with them, he took bread, gave thanks, broke it and began to give it to them. Then their eyes were opened and they recognized him" (Luke 24:30-31). Did you catch that? It was only in the intimacy of breaking bread together that "their eyes were opened."

Step Eleven drives us to "conscious contact with God." The road to this "conscious contact" is actually pretty simple: prayer and meditation. It's not that complicated. Scripture tells us that children came to Jesus openly and freely, full of expectation and life. If you wait until you fully understand the God of the universe before you talk to the God of the universe, it will never happen. The key to lighting a room is flipping a switch, not understanding electricity. The key to Step Eleven is prayer and meditation, not an advanced degree in theology.

LESSON 5: GOD'S REVELATION IS PROGRESSIVE.

No one ever responds to God the first time. There is usually a period of doubt, analysis, and trial and error that comes first. There is a reason Step Eleven comes toward the end, rather than the beginning of the 12-Step process. By definition, "improve" (your conscious contact with God) implies process. The example of the Emmaus Road experience lays this out for us.

1. **They walked without God**. We read, "Now that same day two of them were going to a village called Emmaus, about seven miles from Jerusalem" (Luke 24:13). That is the first phase in our relationship with God. No one is born a Christ-follower. We walk without God.

2. **They were joined by God but did not know it.** "As they talked and discussed these things with each other, Jesus himself came up and walked along with them; but they were kept from recognizing him" (Luke 24:15-16).

3. **They were attracted to Jesus**. After Jesus had walked a good distance with them, we read, "As they approached the village to which they were going, Jesus continued on as if he were going further. But they urged him strongly, 'Stay with us, for it is nearly evening; the day is almost over.' So he went in to stay with them" (Luke 24:28-29). The two men didn't even know their new friend was Jesus, but there was something about him that attracted them. They wanted to know more. This is the third phase.

4. **They embraced God**. "Then their eyes were opened and they recognized him" (Luke

24:31). The process is really never over. The more we seek, the more we find.

LESSON 6: RECOVERY MAY NOT BEGIN WITH JESUS, BUT IT ENDS THERE.

Seven of the 12 steps refer to a Higher Power or spiritual connection. Since the only requirement for membership in a SA or SAA fellowship is "a desire to stop acting out," it is not required to connect with God to begin the 12-Step process. There is a Higher Power theme throughout the Steps: an admission of powerlessness (Step One); belief in a Power greater than ourselves (Step Two); a decision to turn our lives over to the care of God (Step Three); an admission to God of our personal defects (Step Five); a readiness to have God remove these defects (Step Six); and a prayer for him to do so (Step Seven). But none of these steps identify who this Higher Power is.

For some, the 12-Step group becomes their Higher Power. For others, it is some form of mysticism or vague consciousness. And we must respect that.

But we have to be clear here. Each of these examples—the group, mystic thought, etc.—are forms of power, but they are not the *Higher Power*. They will start you down the road to recovery, but they will not get you all the way home.

The road to Emmaus began in Jerusalem, the heart of religion. From there the two men walked a long and winding road. At no point did they deny a

Higher Power. To the contrary, it was their faith that had them in Jerusalem in the first place. But then something happened that rocked their universe.

Jesus joined them in their journey. By the time they broke bread with the Master, "their eyes were opened" (Luke 24:31). They ran back to Jerusalem and told the disciples, "It is true! The Lord has risen" (Luke 24:34).

Succinctly, anything less than a resurrected Savior is the wrong Higher Power. Recovery begins in your bottom-line behaviors, in your darkest valley. On this pathway you can experience sobriety and a level of sanity you never knew before. But to reach the mountaintop, you need the help of the one who has been there. His name is Jesus Christ. No other "Higher Power" will do.

LESSON 7: RECOVERY ALWAYS INCLUDES A LEVEL OF HEARTBURN.

The men said to themselves, "Were not our hearts burning within us while he talked to us on the road and opened the Scriptures to us?" (Luke 24:32). Anyone with successful recovery will tell you the same thing. Recovery brings heartburn. Acknowledging one's insanity, powerlessness, and utter despair is disconcerting, at the least. Facing one's character defects, making amends, and charting a whole new course will shake the addict to his feet. Why?

We always prefer the problem we know over the solution we don't know.

The addict always seeks a softer, easier way. He doesn't want to go to meetings, see a therapist, or give a full clinical disclosure to his wife.

I remember the day I gave my disclosure to Beth. Of course, it was traumatizing to her. But it was perhaps my most painful moment, as well. Confessing your sins, living outside your head, and charting a new course will bring heartburn. It's good heartburn, but it still burns.

LESSON 8: RECOVERY FOLLOWS A PREDICTABLE PATTERN.

Ralph Waldo Emerson said, "Our greatest glory is not in never falling, but in rising up every time we fail."[5] Unfortunately, recovery is not a linear journey. I have yet to meet the man who woke up one day and said, "Ok! I'm ready for recovery," and then began a lifelong upward climb, void of slips, relapses, or struggles. There is always a period of figuring things out, trial and error, and adapting to the challenges of sobriety.

The men on the Emmaus Road demonstrated this pattern for us. The six simple steps in their process of figuring it all out apply to every recovery story I know.

1. **We hear it**. Cleopas and his buddy had heard it already. They discussed what they had

seen and heard (Luke 24:14-15). When Jesus joined their journey, they told him the things they had heard (Luke 24:19-24). Clearly, they had been taught about Jesus, and even by Jesus. But it did not stick. Likewise, when we enter our first recovery meetings, we hear principles of sobriety, but they rarely stick at first.

2. **We give up on it**. When times became difficult, when life didn't make sense, the guys walked away. They checked out of Jerusalem and the whole "Jesus thing." They were done. That's how so many of us were in early recovery. I see it all the time: addict comes into a 12-Step meeting, addict listens, then addict finds recovery to be difficult. So addict gives up, at least for a while.

3. **We hear it again**. Jesus joined the two men. He told them the same things they had already heard (Luke 24:25-27). Jesus knew we rarely get it the first time. That's why SA and SAA groups encourage new attendees to come to at least six meetings.

4. **We understand it**. "Their eyes were opened" (Luke 24:31). It took me a long time to understand the power of surrender and the need for accountability. I had to hear about recovery, read about recovery, and see recovery in others. That is true for all of us. If we stay

in recovery long enough, it starts to make sense.

5. **We embrace it**. The two men responded to Jesus' presence and to his words. That's how it works in recovery, as well. When we finally embrace the principles of recovery, working the steps, and working our program, we get well.

6. **We give it away**. After breaking bread with Jesus, "they got up and returned at once to Jerusalem" (Luke 24:32). This is the final piece of the puzzle—helping others. And it is the inevitable result of true recovery.

LESSON 9: THE MEASURE OF THE ELEVENTH STEP IS WORKING THE TWELFTH STEP.

"They got up and returned at once to Jerusalem. There they found the Eleven and those with them, assembled together and saying, 'It is true! The Lord has risen and has appeared to Simon.' Then the two told what had happened on the way, and how Jesus was recognized by them when he broke the bread" (Luke 24:33-35).

There is only one way to measure the success of working Step Eleven—moving quickly to Step Twelve. Once they made conscious contact with God, the two men were ready to take their message to the world. They had several reasons to stay the night in Emmaus, get some rest, and then head back to Jerusalem the next day: (a) it would be a seven-mile walk, (b) they had already walked seven miles, (c) it was late, (d) they weren't packed for another overnight stay.

You can help others without first having a spiritual connection. But you can't have a spiritual connection and then not help others. When I attend 12-Step meetings out of town, I can generally tell which guys are doing well in recovery because they are the ones who are reaching out to newcomers, sponsoring others, and living beyond themselves.

BREAKING DOWN THE ELEVENTH STEP

Blaise Pascal said, "If God exists, not seeking him must be the gravest error imaginable. If one decides to sincerely seek God and doesn't find God, the lost effort is negligible in comparison to what is at risk in not seeking God in the first place."[6]

What Bill W. and Dr. Bob wrote 80 years ago still holds today. From the experience of their own recovery and encounters with God, they wrote, *"We sought through prayer and meditation to improve our conscious contact with God as we understood him, praying only for knowledge of his will for us and the power to carry it out."*

The men on the Emmaus Road experienced their version of the Eleventh Step. It's hard to imagine a step that is more aligned with the teachings of Christ. So let's break it down, one phrase at a time.

WE SOUGHT

God blesses seekers. The Bible is full of those "who sought." Moses sought God in the wilderness, Jacob sought God in Bethel, the wise men sought God in the cradle, and Paul sought God in the desert. We are promised that if we seek God we will find him (Jeremiah 29:13). This is where the Step Eleven begins—by seeking. Apologist William Lane Craig said, "If you're sincerely seeking God, God will make his existence evident to you."[7]

THROUGH PRAYER AND MEDITATION

Prayer is both a means and an end. Step Eleven teaches us to pray in order to achieve something—in this case, conscious contact with God. But prayer "just" for the sake of prayer is a worthy exercise. The disciples asked Jesus to teach them "to pray," not "how to pray." The sister of prayer is meditation. This is the practice of setting aside time to focus intentionally on the things of God and his will for our lives. Prayer and meditation—these are the vehicles by which we find and maintain conscious contact with God.

TO IMPROVE

Billy Graham once referred to his life as a "failure." All of us have room to grow. By the time we get to the Eleventh Step, we have likely established contact with God. But Step Eleven teaches us to *improve* this contact, to take it to a higher level. This is one of the gifts of recovery—a constant drive to improve.

OUR CONSCIOUS CONTACT WITH GOD

We must be careful to keep our eyes on the prize. In today's worship culture, for example, there seems to be a premium on establishing the right atmosphere or experience. I love what Rick Warren says about this: "The most common mistake Christians make in worship today is seeking an experience rather than seeking God."[8] We are not to seek the experience that God gives, but the God who gives experiences.

PRAYING FOR KNOWLEDGE OF HIS WILL

The Step goes further. As we seek contact with God, we do so with a purpose. Our prayer is one for knowledge of God's will. We can't do God's will until we know God's will. This comes through the Word, wise counsel, and prayer.

AND THE POWER TO CARRY THAT OUT

Knowing God's will is far less important than doing God's will. This is hard for many addicts, as we tend to feel a lot of shame. Billy Graham advised, "Don't let your past mistakes keep you from seeking God." One of the gifts of our addiction is this life lesson—we are powerless. For the addict, asking God for the power to follow through with right choices is natural, as we know that apart from that power we don't have a chance.

By now, you have read the Eleventh Step dozens of times. You may have even memorized it. Now let's add the Eleventh Step Prayer to your repertoire as you seek to improve your conscious contact with God.

> *"Lord, make me an instrument of thy peace!*
> *That where there is hatred, I may bring love.*
> *That where there is wrong, I may bring the*
> *spirit of forgiveness."*

STEP TWELVE

BROTHER ANDREW

JOHN 1:40-42

"Having had a spiritual awakening as a result of these steps, we tried to carry this message to other alcoholics, and to practice these principles in all our affairs."

Neil Diamond had ten *Billboard* #1 hits. But it was another song that didn't rise to such esteem on the charts that speaks to the Twelfth Step—*Brother Love's Traveling Salvation Show*. This 1969 song includes the following lyrics.

> *Hallelujah, brothers*
> *Halle-hallelujah*
> *I said brothers.*
> *Now you got yourself two good hands*
> *And when your brother is troubled,*
> *You gotta reach out your one hand for him*
> *'Cause that's what it's there for.*
> *And when your heart is troubled,*
> *You gotta reach out your other hand,*

Reach it out to the man up there
'Cause that's what he's there for.[1]

We work the 12 Steps with two hands—one extended toward God and the other extended toward others. Early in our recovery we find ourselves barely holding on. While reaching up to God with one hand, we use our other hand to grab hold of a group, sponsor, literature—anything that can help us dig out of the hole in which we find ourselves. But as we work the steps, we come to Step Twelve more organically than systematically. It just happens. The final step tells us to give back, and we do it—not because the step tells us to, but because this is what feels natural.

The AA Big Book says, "The joy of living is the theme of AA's Twelfth Step, and action is the key word."[2] While other Steps are more contemplative, this one is all about action. It's about giving back. To quote St. Augustine, "What does love look like? It has hands to help others. It has feet to hasten to the poor and needy. It has eyes to see misery and want. It has ears to hear the sighs and sorrows of men. That is what love looks like."[3]

The first chapter of John introduces us to Jesus' "Traveling Salvation Show." It was during those travels that he encountered the original Twelfth-stepper, a man named Andrew. While Andrew's more famous brother became the "rock" on which Jesus would build his church, it was only through Andrew's working of the Twelfth Step that this became possible.

THE TRAVELING SALVATION SHOW

"Andrew, Simon Peter's brother, was one of the two who heard what John had said and who had followed Jesus. The first thing Andrew did was to find his brother Simon and tell him, 'We have found the Messiah' (that is, the Christ). And he brought him to Jesus. Jesus looked at him and said, 'You are Simon son of John. You will be called Cephas' (which, when translated, is Peter)" (John 1:40-42).

This Twelfth Step story consists of four characters. While our primary interest for our purposes will focus on the life of Andrew, his story cannot be told in isolation.

JOHN THE BAPTIST

Before Andrew was a follower of Christ, he was a follower of John the Baptist. For those unsure of the legacy of this unusual prophet, Jesus settles the issue with one sentence: "Truly I tell you, among those born of woman, there has risen no one greater than John the Baptist" (Matthew 11:11). The Gospels tell us the story of this amazing man. This is what we know.

Matthew tells us that John emerged from the wilderness, preaching a message of repentance. He proclaimed the coming of the Messiah. John had camel's hair for his clothing and locusts as his main course. He referred to religious leaders as "vipers."

Mark adds that John preached "the baptism of repentance."

Luke tells us that John's ministry occurred during the time when Pontius Pilate was governor of Judaea. Luke also details John's message with amazing examples of imagery.

John, the writer of the fourth Gospel, described John the Baptist as "a man sent from God." He identified his mission as "bearing witness of the Light, that all men through him might believe."

The ministry of John the Baptist began about six months before that of Jesus and ended with his imprisonment and beheading. He had several students who took note of his every word and supported his ministry. Among these students—called "disciples"— were Andrew and Peter.

ANDREW

We don't know a lot about Andrew. History tells us he was born in 5 B.C. in the region of Galilee, in the village of Bethsaida. His name was Greek, not Hebrew, which was not unusual in that area. "Andrew" means *manly* or *brave*. Andrew was a professional fisherman; hence, Jesus called him to be a "fisher of men."

John's Gospel tells us that Andrew was a disciple of John the Baptist. When he became a follower of Christ, he demonstrated passionate servanthood from the beginning. Like his mentor, Andrew was content to live in second place, always in the shadow of his brother. In fact, he was most often referred to as "Simon Peter's brother." Andrew was never in the inner circle, and was therefore excluded from such events as the Transfiguration, raising of Jairus' daughter, and the Garden prayer. But Andrew did what he was created for—consistently, throughout his life.

Following the ascension of Christ, Andrew continued to do what he did best—point men to the faith that had saved his life. The historian Eusebius quoted the ancient historian Origen in *Church History*, as saying that Andrew preached in Scythia.[4] *The Chronicle of Nestor* adds that he preached near the Black Sea, then traveled to the land that would eventually become Romania. Tradition says that he was martyred for his faith in Patras in Achaia. Condemned to death by crucifixion, he said that he was not worthy to die "as did my Lord." His wish was granted, and he was crucified upside down.[5]

If Andrew had carried a copy of the 12 Steps with him, it is likely that he would have highlighted Steps Three and Twelve. These epitomize the life that Andrew lived.

1. **Andrew worked the Third Step**. Andrew made a decision to turn his will and life over to the care of God as he understood God. The fourth Gospel tells us that "Andrew, Si-

mon Peter's brother, was one of the two who heard what John (the Baptist) had said and who had followed Jesus" (John 1:40). Andrew didn't mess around. He went from Step One to Step Three in record time. Leaving his fishing nets, family, and lifestyle behind, he dropped everything in surrender to Jesus.

2. **Andrew worked the Twelfth Step**. Having had a spiritual awakening as a result of these steps, Andrew carried this message to other fishermen, and practiced these principles in all his affairs. We see several examples of Andrew working the Twelfth Step. First, we read, "The first thing Andrew did was to find his brother Simon and tell him, 'We have found the Messiah.' And he brought him to Jesus" (John 1:41-42). Second, when the 5,000 needed food, it was Andrew who brought the boy with a sack lunch to Jesus (John 6:8-9). Third, it was Andrew who connected the curious Greeks to Jesus when he heard they were seekers of truth (John 12:22).

PETER

In Simon Peter, we see the result of one man working the Twelfth Step. If Andrew had stopped with Step Eleven, Peter would not have been introduced to the Messiah. (We never know the impact we have on others by working the 12 Steps.) One of the best ways to summarize Peter's life is within the context of recovery. We have already seen Peter as a Ninth-stepper, but let's pull back and see a broader picture.

1. **Peter's life before recovery**: He was a common fisherman. We don't know much else. We can assume Peter had been married, as he had a mother-in-law (Matthew 8). Beyond that, we know that he worked alongside his brother, Andrew. As for his faith, he was a disciple of John the Baptist. He was in an ideal place to meet his Higher Power.

2. **How Peter came into recovery**: When Peter heard Jesus speak, he followed him, in order to hear more (John 1:37). He went so far as to ask Jesus where he was staying (John 1:38). His time with the Lord was so impactful that the actual time of day was recorded—4:00 p.m. (the Jewish "tenth hour"). Jesus welcomed Peter into his developing inner circle of closest confidants because he saw beyond who Peter was into the future of who he would become.

3. **Peter's life after recovery**: Jesus saw who Peter was, but especially who he would become. That's why he gave him a new name. First, he was known as "Simon." This was a common Hebraic name meaning "listen-

er." Then, Jesus said his name would be "Cephas," which was Aramaic, the common language of the day and the language, which Jesus spoke. Finally, he would also be known as "Peter," which was the equivalent of "Cephas" in Greek, meaning "rock." Was Peter a rock early on? Hardly! But that was exactly what he would become—after Jesus' recovery work had been completed in his life. (Andrew jumped to Step Twelve quickly; it took Peter until Acts 2.)

JESUS

Jesus is for you. He is presented as the Messiah (Hebrew) and Christ (Greek). Both titles refer to one who is anointed by God. In the ancient world, kings were anointed with oil at their coronations. "Messiah" and "Christos" both literally mean "God's anointed King."

Without Jesus there is no real recovery. We see Jesus bringing recovery to the lives of both brothers—Andrew and Peter—in three ways. And what he did for them he will do for us. Jesus (a) sees us as we are, (b) envisions what we can become, and (c) does for us what we could not do for ourselves.

1.   **Jesus sees us as we are**. "Jesus looked at him" (John 1:42). The word for "looked" is *emblepein*, which means to gaze with great

concentration. It means to look into one's heart. When Jesus sees us, he peeks behind the mask, beyond the performance and into the person. This is where recovery always begins—not with us seeing Jesus, but with Jesus seeing us.

2. **Jesus envisions what we can become**. William Barclay said it like this: "He sees not only the actualities, but also the possibilities."[6] Jesus looked at Peter and saw in him not only a Galilean fisherman, but one who had it in him to become the rock on which the church would be built. Jesus sees us not only as we are, but as we can be, and he says, "Give your life to me, and I will make you what you were created to be."

3. **Jesus does for us what we could not do for ourselves**. I love the example of Michelangelo. One day, a man approached him and found the great sculptor chipping away with his chisel at a huge shapeless piece of rock. He asked the great sculptor what he was doing. "I am releasing the angel imprisoned in this marble," he answered. Jesus is the one who sees and can release the hidden angel in every man.

THE TWELFTH STEP—HOW IT WORKS

Ronald Reagan said, "Let us ask ourselves, 'What kind of people do we think we are?' And let us answer, 'Free people, worthy of freedom and determined not only to remain so but to help others gain their freedom as well.'"[7]

That is the essence of the Twelfth Step. That is what people of recovery are: free people who are not only determined to remain free, but to help others gain their freedom as well. The Twelfth Step is the one we must never put down.

I remember my first several 12-Step meetings. I was pretty miserable. It wasn't that I rejected the tenets of the meetings or the need for recovery. I just didn't like sitting there, watching everyone else do all the readings, make all the announcements, and enjoy all the fellowship. I was the outsider.

But it didn't have to remain that way. By the third month or so, I was at a crossroads. I would either go all in or get out. But I soon realized that "going all in" meant more than just showing up. I began welcoming newcomers, sharing my story, and building relationships. And suddenly, recovery took root.

Carol Burnett said that helping others "is also selfish because it makes you feel good when you help others. I've been helped by acts of kindness from strangers. That's why we're here, after all, to help others."[8]

I've known the value of working Step Twelve for years—experientially. I knew it worked for me, that it helped to cement my personal recovery. But science actually validates the Twelfth Step. A recent study was conducted by Columbia University. It concluded the following. "When helping others navigate their stressful situations, we are enhancing our own emotional regulation skills, and thus, benefiting our own emotional well-being."[9]

We know that the Twelfth Step works. It is an essential part of recovery. To work the first eleven steps, then take our foot off the accelerator is to abort our personal recovery. It's time to break it down. How does the Final Step work, exactly?

A SPIRITUAL AWAKENING

Step Twelve begins, "Having had a spiritual awakening as a result of these steps..." As we have seen, seven of the 12 steps refer directly to spirituality: Steps 2, 3, 5, 6, 7, 11, and 12. You cannot work the 12 steps apart from the help of your Higher Power. And we would argue, of course, that the *Highest Power* is Jehovah God, known through his Son Jesus Christ. The Twelfth Step compels us to carry the message of recovery, but we cannot carry this message apart from our spiritual connection. In *Step into Action*, a book that serves as a template for leading someone through the steps, we read, "Our spiritual awaking propels us to carry the message to the sexaholic who still suffers."[10]

CARRYING THE MESSAGE

Dr. Marianny Pogosyan, writing for *Psychology Today*, wrote, "There is now neural evidence from fMRI studies suggesting a link between generosity and happiness in the brain. Helping others regulate their emotions helps us regulate our own emotions, decreases symptoms of depression and ultimately improves our own."[11]

In other words, when we help others, we help ourselves. "Carrying the message" is as much of a parallel statement for the Steps and the Gospel as there is. In the Gospels, carrying the message is both a command and an instinct.

Sharing the Good News is the Great Commandment (Matthew 28:19-20). This was the last thing Jesus told us to do—"Be my witnesses" (Acts 1:8). But "carrying the message" was also an instinctive reaction among early converts. Legion told ten cities, the paralytic told his friends, and as we have already seen, Andrew told his brother. The early disciples couldn't seem to help themselves. We find at least 40 miracles in the Gospels. Repeatedly, the person who was healed immediately told someone else.

The world of psychology provides more evidence of the benefits of working the Twelfth Step. Research presented at the 2017 Society for Personality and Social Psychology Annual Convention found that when we share good news with others, we receive benefits from it as well, including more restful sleep, clearer communication, and better emotional support.[12]

But we must consider a warning when working the Twelfth Step. I suggest it is possible to "overwork" the Final Step. Let me illustrate.

One of the things I most enjoy in both of my home 12-Step meetings is welcoming newcomers. When I see a newcomer, I remember what it was like for me when I walked through those doors for the first time. (I was terrified, mortified, and petrified!) So I quickly introduce myself to the newcomer, introduce him to others, hand him literature, sit with him, and offer to exchange cell numbers. And all of that is good. But here's the mistake I have made too often—*trying to carry the addict rather than simply carrying the message*. One of Dad's favorite Bible verses was, "You can lead a horse to water, but you can't make him drink." (At least he said that was in the Bible!)

You obviously can't complete the 12 Steps without working the Final Step. And at the heart of this step are these three simple words: "carrying the message." Andrew carried the message. You can find sobriety without carrying the message, but not recovery. Every true spiritual awakening will motivate you to carry the message. But there's more . . .

PRACTICE THESE PRINCIPLES IN ALL OUR AFFAIRS

I rarely turn to the world of college basketball for recovery inspiration, but it's always good to make an exception with the "Wizard of Westwood," John Wooden. Generally recognized as the greatest college basketball coach in history, Wooden led UCLA to ten national championships in twelve years. But he understood life even better than basketball. Wooden said, "Be true to yourself, help others, make each day your masterpiece, make friendship a fine art, drink deeply from good books—especially the Bible, build a shelter against a rainy day, give thanks for your blessings and pray for guidance every day."[13]

Coach Wooden was basically saying to live a life of integrity. The idea of "practicing these principles" is consistent with the teachings of Christ, who had a lot to say about the process of discipleship. For Jesus, salvation was an event ("You must be born again"), but it was also a process. The transformation offered through the resurrected Christ (2 Corinthians 5:20) is one of process: "Be continually transformed."

With Step Twelve there must be a warning. Never assume that because you have completed the 12 Steps, you have completed recovery. As we've said before, regardless how far you have come, the ditch on either side of the road is still just as close.

May the same ethic of the men who built God's house of old be our ethic in working Step Twelve. "So the workmen labored, and the repair work progressed in their hands, and they restored the house of God according to its specifications and strengthened it" (2 Chronicles 24:13).

The 12 Steps are God's specifications. As we take the journey, may He strengthen us now.

CONCLUSION

B etty Ford once admitted, "I knew I was an alcoholic because I was preoccupied with whether
alcohol was going to be served or not."[1] For me, I knew
I had a problem when I found myself violating my own
personal code—for years. The pattern became as consistent as it was predictable: I thought it, I planned it,
I did it, I hated it, I covered it, and then I did it again. I
sought help through prayer, counseling, more prayer,
and more counseling.

But it was the principles of the 12 Steps that
saved me. That's because this is a spiritual program,
rooted in biblical principles and a connection to God,
as established by the founders of Alcoholics Anonymous 80 years ago.

We must never put the Steps on the level of dei-
ty. I did not find God through recovery; I found recovery through God. But I have discovered that God uses
the same principles that he created in the genesis of
it all—such as surrender, honesty, and amends. And
these principles are delineated in the Steps.

We have seen each of the steps come alive in
Scripture, through Jesus' real encounters with real
men and women. If, by the reading of this book, you

have come to a fuller understanding of the integration of Scripture and the Steps, my goal will have been met. Then, by working these steps—with the Bible in one hand and recovery material in the other—your goals will be met.

If you are an addict, or are married to one, don't walk this path alone. Find a 12-Step group in your area, or at least online. Reach out to us at **TheresStillHope. org**. We have resources, coaching, and groups that can make a difference.

Are you in need of personal sobriety and recovery? It all starts with Step One. It can start today.

APPENDIX A

STATISTICS ON SEX ADDICTION

All Cited in My Book, 'Porn in the Pew'[1]

The General Porn Problem

- Porn is a $12 billion industry in the United States.
- The top porn site had 23 billion visits in 2016.
- 25% of all search engine searches are porn related.
- Porn sites receive more visits than Netflix, Amazon, and Twitter combined.
- Child porn is a $3 billion industry in the United States.
- 40 million Americans view porn regularly.
- On average, the first view of porn occurs at age 11.
- 90% of children ages 8-16 have viewed porn on the Internet.
- 71% of porn use is online.
- 35% of all Internet downloads are porn related.

- There are 4.2 million porn websites.
- Hotel adult film viewership is 55%.
- Between 10 and 18% of men admit to a sexual addiction.
- While the U.S. makes up just 4.3% of the world's population, it represents 12.4% of porn use, three times the world average.
- Porn increases marital infidelity by 300%.

Porn Epidemic in the Church

- 62% of evangelical men view porn monthly, compared to 64% of the general population of men.
- 95% of Christian men have viewed porn.
- 78% of Christian men view porn several times a year.
- 53% of men who attended Promise Keeper meetings viewed porn the next week.
- 13% of Christian men say they are addicted to porn; another 5% say they may be.
- Christian men view porn at work with the same frequency as non-believers.
- 47% of Christian families say porn is a problem in their home.
- The most popular day for Christians to view porn is Sunday.
- 7% of Christians view porn several times a day.
- Over 50% of church staffs struggle with cyber-sex.

- 29% of born-again adults feel porn is morally acceptable.
- 57% of pastors say porn addiction is the most damaging issue in their congregation.

Porn Use Among Clergy

- 54% of pastors have viewed pornography within the past 12 months.
- 37% of pastors admit to a struggle with porn.
- 30% of pastors have viewed porn in the past 30 days.
- 25% of pastors have purchased printed porn.
- 21% of student pastors struggle with porn "right now."
- Among pastors who call the Focus on the Family toll-free helpline, 70% say they are addicted to porn.
- Only 25% of pastors have any form of accountability.

Porn Use Among Sub-Groups

- 62% of all men view porn.
- 50% of men struggle with porn.
- 25% of men hide their Internet browser.
- 79% of men ages 18-30 view porn.
- 67% of men ages 31-49 view porn.
- 49% of men ages 50-68 view porn.
- 33% of millennials say they might be addicted to sex.

- Porn use among women is rising quickly.
- 28% of those admitting to sex addiction are now women.
- 34% of readers of *Today's Christian Women* use Internet porn.
- 20% of women admit to struggling with porn.
- 70% of women view porn regularly.
- 33% of women ages 18-24 view porn regularly.
- 13% of women have accessed porn at work.
- 6% of all Christian women seek porn at least once per month.
- Women are more likely than men to view hard-core porn.
- 18% of Christian women view porn "a few times a year," compared to just 15% among non-Christian women.
- 60% of women have a serious struggle with lust.

APPENDIX B

BRIEF HISTORY OF
SEX ADDICTS ANONYMOUS

Sex Addicts Anonymous was founded in 1977 by a group of men who perceived a personal need for help with their sexually compulsive activities. Though they had found some help through Alcoholics Anonymous groups and material, they sought a higher level of focus on their specific needs, as well as personal anonymity. Since its founding, SAA has grown enormously, with hundreds of meetings throughout all 50 states of the U.S., as well as across Canada.

What Makes SAA Unique

Unlike other programs, SAA is open to those of all sexual orientations. The only condition for membership is a desire to find sobriety. Rooted in the traditions of Alcoholics Anonymous, SAA leans heavily on the "three circles," described below. Also unique among the "S" fellowships is SAA's definition of sobriety. That is left to each participant to decide for himself or herself. Further, it is common in SAA groups to find mixed sexes in attendance, whereas other fellow-ships tend to discourage same sex meetings.

SAA offers a variety of meetings. In addition to the traditional SAA 12-Step meetings, "boundary meetings" are offered for subgroups such as clergy, doctors, and therapists who require more anonymity than others in attendance. Dozens of phone meetings are offered throughout the week, as well, for those unable or unwilling to attend a live meeting.

Though most groups feature the AA "big book" prominently, in every meeting, there will be readings from the "green book," produced specifically by and for SAA. The "green book" follows a similar pattern to AA, including much of its language and the 12 Steps that are recommended to find sobriety.

Sponsors

SAA places a high level of importance on working the Steps and on getting a sponsor early in the program. Newcomers are quickly introduced to the 12-Step program, as most groups display the Steps prominently on a banner or in some other visible way. Newcomers are urged to secure a sponsor quickly, who will begin the process of guiding the new member through the steps. Most SAA groups set their standards high, in terms of who can become a sponsor. It is not uncommon for a group to require a member to achieve one year of sobriety and to have completed all 12 steps before becoming a sponsor.

The Three Circles

Taken from AA, the three circles represent spec-ified activities of active addiction and recovery. With the help of his sponsor, the member will be encour-aged to draw a large circle, with smaller circles en-closed, on a sheet of paper. Then the participant will write into the outer circle those activities which pro-mote his personal sobriety. These activities will gener-ally include attending 12-Step meetings, prayer, work-ing with one's sponsor, and healthy living.

Then he will identify his "middle circle" behav-iors. These are activities that, while not considered a break in technical sobriety, lead the addict in that in-evitable direction, if not curbed. These activities might include certain types of movies, places, and even peo-ple who trigger the addict into a strong desire to "act out." Finally, the inner circle is considered. Here, the addict writes down any activity that breaks his sobri-ety, as he has defined it.

COSA

Formerly known as C.O.S.A. (Co-Sex Addicts or Codependents of Sex Addicts), this is a sister orga-nization to SAA. These are groups for the spouses of sex addicts. They generally conduct meetings once a week, often at the same general location as an SAA meeting. COSA provides connection, fellowship, and encouragement for those married to sex addicts.

APPENDIX C

BRIEF HISTORY OF SEXAHOLICS ANONYMOUS

Sexaholics Anonymous (SA) traces its roots to Roy K., who identified his sobriety date as January 31, 1976. Roy founded SA in the 1970s, and received permission from AA to use its Twelve Steps and Twelve Traditions in 1979. Roy remained active in the program and in his recovery until his death from cancer on September 15, 2009. From its beginning, SA has maintained a strict sobriety definition and has seen multiple challenges to its standards and practices. Still, SA has prospered and spread its message and presence around the world.

What Makes SA Unique

Like SAA, SA utilizes the AA "blue book" in its readings during meetings. And like SAA, SA has produced its own book, referred to as the "white book." It is similar to the SAA "green book," with a similar focus on the 12 Steps and commitment to sobriety.

Perhaps the most significant distinction of SA is its relentless definition of sobriety as not having sex with anyone other than the spouse. In 1991, after a failed attempt to broaden this sobriety definition to allow for same sex couples and those in heterosexual, committed relationships (outside of legal marriage), a group led by Murray R. splintered off to form Sexual Recovery Anonymous (SRA). Another challenge to the traditional definition of sobriety was rejected in the late 1990s.

SA is more closely aligned with AA in its philosophy of sobriety. Just as AA offers a definitive standard of sobriety, SA does not leave this to the individual participants. SA applies AA standards to lust and sexual addiction. Its multiple publications support this standard.

Other Meetings

In addition to its regular meetings, SA has held annual conventions since 1981. The organization also offers phone meetings for those unable to attend "live" meetings. With an expansive selection of supplementary literature, participants are offered extensive resources for outside reading. The *Step into Action* series provides excellent guidance for sponsors as they lead sponsees through the program.

S-Anon

The sister organization to SA, created for spouses of addicts, is S-Anon, which is an anonymous group for spouses. S-Anon follows the same 12-Step formula of AA and SA. While S-Anon traditionally identifies its members as co-addicts or co-dependents, this has become largely rejected by many of its members, who would argue that being married to an addict does not define that person.

APPENDIX D

PRIMARY DIFFERENCES BETWEEN SAA AND SA

Many participants float seamlessly from one fellowship to the other. While some prefer one fellowship over the other, most seem to join a particular fellowship based largely on accessibility. For example, this author attended hundreds of SAA meetings while living in Texas, as SAA is more prominent there. (There are about 60 SAA weekly meetings in the Houston area alone.) But once moving to Florida, it was soon discovered that the opposite is true there, where SA is far more prominent. Having said that, notable differences exist.

Sobriety Definition

As already covered, SAA encourages each member to define his or her own sobriety. As a part of these looser boundaries, SAA provides a more comfortable landing for most women, homosexuals, and men in committed relationships, but not married. For those seeking a more traditional definition of sobriety, SA is a more comfortable fit.

Sobriety Date

When introducing oneself in an SAA meeting, the attendee will state his first name and something of his story. He may include the forms by which he act-ed out. SA offers a distinctive addition. In addition to stating his name, each participant is expected to state his "sobriety date," which usually refers to the last day on which he acted out sexually (outside of marriage). Some prefer this, as it forces each participant to re-main accountable for his sobriety. Others dislike this for of a "check-in," seeing it as (a) putting too much emphasis on a date, and (b) setting those with longer sobriety apart from the rest of the fellowship.

Literature

Both SA and SAA use the AA "blue book," also referred to as the "big book." But more readings are done out of each fellowship's own material. As stated, SAA uses a "green book," which includes great em-phasis on the AA three circles. SA does not use this specific language, but offers other readings that are found equally helpful by many members.

Other Nuances

Upon attending numerous meetings of each fel-lowship, the attendee will likely notice a few other nuanced differences. For example, SAA seems to place a greater emphasis on getting a sponsor early in the program, and on working the 12 steps with great intentionality. SA groups, on the other hand, often place a greater emphasis on specific sobriety dates. They also tend to restrict meetings to members of the same sex, which limits the potential "triggers" that participants might experience in the meetings.

APPENDIX E

CELEBRATE RECOVERY

Millions of Americans have found hope and recovery through the Christ-centered program known as Celebrate Recovery. CR was launched by Saddleback Church, in Lake Forest, California, under the leadership of founding pastor Rick Warren. That was in 1991, when Saddleback was still meeting in a high school gym.

The founder of CR was John Baker, who still serves in leadership decades later. In 1991, Baker wrote a 13-page letter to Warren, laying out his vision for the ministry. Warren was happy to turn him loose. And Celebrate Recovery began.

For its first meeting, 43 were in attendance. Initially, CR had four "Open Share Groups"—Men's and Women's Chemical Dependency and Men's and Women's Codependency. Since her early days, CR now offers 14 specific groups. At Saddleback alone, over 27,000 individuals have participated in the program.

Today, there are over 35,000 churches around the globe that have hosted Celebrate Recovery groups. Publications such as *Step Studies, The Journey Begins*, and *The Journey Continues* provide substantive work for each group member.

Despite its profound impact, Celebrate Recovery is not without its critics. It does have at least two specific limitations.

Not an Addiction Program

Though CR is widely viewed as an addiction recovery program, the materials make no such claim. From the very beginning, CR was established to offer hope to those with "hurts, habits, and hang-ups." While these terms certainly include the challenges of addiction, they do not specify this. Thus, the CR program is too broad to bring laser focus to the challenge of porn or sex addiction.

Few "S" Meetings

After the initial joint worship and testimony time, participants are directed to their focused groups. Theoretically, there will be meetings for those who struggle with alcohol, drugs, food, sex, etc. The problem is that most meetings are too small to offer a significant breakout group for sex addicts. And sex addicts are no longer anonymous when they have to self-identify as such in the larger meeting.

Long Meetings

While there are exceptions, most SA and SAA meetings last 60 minutes. The meeting facilitators are strict about enforcing this standard. On the other hand, CR meetings usually require 90 minutes. Many potential attendees prefer shorter meetings.

APPENDIX F

THE TWELVE STEPS OF ALCOHOLICS ANONYMOUS

1. We admitted that we were powerless over alcohol—that our lives had become unmanageable.
2. Came to believe that a Power greater than ourselves could restore us to sanity.
3. Made a decision to turn our will and our lives over to the care of God as we understood Him.
4. Made a searching and fearless moral inventory of ourselves.
5. Admitted to God, to ourselves, and to another human being the exact nature of our wrongs.
6. Were entirely ready to have God remove all these defects of character.
7. Humbly asked Him to remove our shortcomings.
8. Made a list of all persons we had harmed, and became willing to make amends to them all.
9. Made direct amends to such people whenever possible, except when to do so would injure them or others.

10. Continued to take personal inventory and when we were wrong promptly admitted it.

11. Sought through prayer and meditation to improve our conscious contact with God, as we understood Him, praying only for knowledge of His will for us, and the power to carry that out.

12. Having had a spiritual awakening as the result of these Steps, we tried to carry this message to alcoholics, and to practice these principles in all our affairs.

APPENDIX G

THE TWELVE STEPS OF SEXAHOLICS ANONYMOUS

1. We admitted that we were powerless over lust—that our lives had become unmanageable.
2. Came to believe that a Power greater than ourselves could restore us to sanity.
3. Made a decision to turn our will and our lives over to the care of God as we understood Him.
4. Made a searching and fearless moral inventory of ourselves.
5. Admitted to God, to ourselves, and to another human being the exact nature of our wrongs.
6. Were entirely ready to have God remove all these defects of character.
7. Humbly asked Him to remove our shortcomings.
8. Made a list of all persons we had harmed, and became willing to make amends to them all.
9. Made direct amends to such people wherever possible, except when to do so would injure them or others.

10. Continued to take personal inventory and when we were wrong, promptly admitted it.

11. Sought through prayer and meditation to improve our conscious contact with God as we understood Him, praying only for knowledge of His will for us and the power to carry that out.

12. Having had a spiritual awakening as the result of these Steps, we tried to carry this message to sexaholics, and to practice these principles in all our affairs.

APPENDIX H

THE TWELVE STEPS OF SEX ADDICTS ANONYMOUS

1. We admitted we were powerless over addictive sexual behavior—that our lives had become unmanageable.
2. Came to believe that a Power greater than ourselves could restore us to sanity.
3. Made a decision to turn our will and our lives over to the care of God as we understood God.
4. Made a searching and fearless moral inventory of ourselves.
5. Admitted to God, to ourselves, and to another human being the exact nature of our wrongs.
6. Were entirely ready to have God remove all these defects of character.
7. Humbly asked God to remove our shortcomings.
8. Made a list of all persons we had harmed and became willing to make amends to them all.
9. Made direct amends to such people wherever possible, except when to do so would injure them or others.

10. Continued to take personal inventory and when we were wrong promptly admitted it.

11. Sought through prayer and meditation to improve our conscious contact with God as we understood God, praying only for knowledge of God's will for us and the power to carry that out.

12. Having had a spiritual awakening as the result of these Steps, we tried to carry this message to other sex addicts and to practice these principles in our lives.

APPENDIX I

THE TWELVE STEPS OF CELEBRATE RECOVERY

1. We admitted we were powerless over our addictions and compulsive behaviors, that our lives had become unmanageable.
2. We came to believe that a power greater than ourselves could restore us to sanity.
3. We made a decision to turn our lives and our wills over to the care of God.
4. We made a searching and fearless moral inventory of ourselves.
5. We admitted to God, to ourselves, and to another human being the exact nature of our wrongs.
6. We were entire ready to have God remove all these defects of character.
7. We humbly asked Him to remove all our shortcomings.
8. We made a list of all persons we had harmed and became willing to make amends to them all.

9. We made direct amends to such people whenever possible, except when to do so would injure them or others.
10. We continued to take personal inventory, and when we were wrong, promptly admitted it.
11. We sought through prayer and meditation to improve our conscious contact with God, praying only for knowledge of His will and the power to carry that out.
12. Having had a spiritual awakening as a result of these steps, we tried to carry this message to others and to practice these principles in all our affairs.

APPENDIX J

CRITICISM OF THE TWELVE STEPS

As successful as the Steps have been in facilitating sobriety for millions of people around the world, the Steps are not without their critics. While membership in Alcoholics Anonymous groups has expanded to 2.1 million people meeting in 114,000 groups, many still find fault with the "one size fits all" approach.[1]

Therapists seem to support 12-Step programs on the whole. A 2014 study found that nearly 80% of clinicians surveyed had referred clients to 12-Step groups.[2] Still, there are several arguments that have been suggested, which undercut the credibility of the Steps as a reliable plan of sobriety. While this author is a stanch proponent of the Steps, it would be a disservice to our readers to not offer a brief summation of the criticisms of the Steps.

THIN EMPIRICAL EVIDENCE

Melanie Storrusten, a noted psychotherapist whose practice is largely focused on issues of addiction, notes that empirical evidence of successful recovery is not easily produced. She said, "What we do have is anecdotal evidence of the many people that groups like AA have helped, including many within the treatment industry, who are not providing treatment."[3]

There is not a strong answer to the "lack of empirical evidence" argument. By the nature of the disease, research on its healing is not easy to track. However, specific treatment plans, such as the 90-Day Recovery Program offered through our ministry, There's Still Hope, have been adapted according to the observations of leaders and clients. There are simply too many men and women who have experienced personal recovery as a result of the Steps and various 12-Step programs to dismiss their success.

FOCUS ON HIGHER POWER

Some find the emphasis on a "Higher Power" limiting. Some readily embrace the spiritual components of recovery quickly; others never get there. Critics of the Steps argue that by demanding an adherence to a "Higher Power," the program is denying its other benefits to those who are truly in need of recovery, but are not deists. Critics suggest that those in need of sobriety take the aspects of the Steps that work for them, then utilize other components of recovery found in yoga, meditation, fitness activities, and engagement with "spiritual" groups that do not tie their spirituality to a literal God.

There can be no response to this criticism that the atheist will accept. To deny the spiritual component of recovery is to invalidate the essence of the process. We have pointed out several times that a majority of the Steps speak directly of God or a "Higher Power." A common theme in recovery is, "Without God, you can't; without you, God won't." While there is great encouragement and benefit from the Steps apart from the power of God, recovery is dependent on God.

POWERLESSNESS EXCUSES RESPONSIBILITY

There is a strong emphasis in all 12-Step groups that suggests the addict is powerless to find sobriety on his own. Critics argue that by telling an addict, starting with Step One, that he lacks the power to confront his disease, AA, SA, or SAA are excusing bad behavior.[4]

The problem with this argument is that the Steps do not suggest that the addict is incapable of recovery. The very nature of the Steps suggests that for every addict there is hope. The Steps then lay out specific actionable responses that lead to sobriety. When 12-Step adherents speak of powerlessness, they are simply saying that the solution is bigger than the addict, but it still includes the participation of the addict.

LOSS OF INDIVIDUALIZED CARE

Storrusten suggests, "I believe that the best care is individualized care."[5] It is true that many who embrace 12-Step groups migrate away from personal therapy. To the degree that any group becomes a substitute for personalized care, that group is doing a disservice to its adherents.

In response, anyone who attends 12-Step meetings for even a few times will quickly see that most participants are also actively involved in personalized therapy. In fact, it is often his therapist who directs the addict to the 12-Step meetings in the first place. The relationship between therapy and the Steps is not either/or, but both/and.

12-STEP MEETINGS BECOME A SUBSTITUTE ADDICTION

It is not uncommon to hear meeting participants voice extremely strong reliance on their groups. Many will credit their group as the most significant component of their sobriety plan. It is not unusual for addicts to attend 90 meetings in 90 days, and to get "hooked" on recovery groups. The critic would suggest that this is merely a new addiction, and not just a means of escape from the old one.

In response, it must be pointed out that everyone needs support. I have yet to find the woman who saw her husband's reliance on 12-Step meetings as intolerable as his reliance on pornography. In treating disease, it is sometimes necessary to prescribe a response that must be carried out for life.

APPENDIX K

RESOURCES

12-Step Programs for Sex Addicts

- Sexaholics Anonymous (SA), 866-424-8777, www.sa.org
- Sex Addicts Anonymous (SAA), 800-477-8191, www.sexaa.org
- Sex and Love Addicts Anonymous (SLAA), 210-828-7900, www.slaafws.org
- Sexual Compulsives Anonymous (SCA), 800-977-4325, www.sca-recovery.org
- Sexual Recovery Anonymous (SRA), 646-450-9690, www.sexualrecovery.org

12-Step Programs for Spouses of Sex Addicts

- S-Anon, 615-833-3152, www.sanon.org
- Co-Dependents of Sex Addicts (COSA), 866-899-2672, www.cosa-recovery.org
- Infidelity Survivors Anonymous (ISA), www.isurvivors.org

Couples Recovery

- Recovering Couples Anonymous (RCA), 877-663-2317, www.recovering-couples.org

Hope & Freedom Counseling Services

- Individualized three-day intensives for couples and for men
- Special programs for physicians and clergy
- Celebrity intensives in the Canadian Rockies
- Contact: 713-630-0111, www.hopeandfreedom.com

Certified Hope & Freedom Practitioners (CHFP)

- These sex addiction therapists are certified in the Hope & Freedom intensive treatment model and offer intensives in various locations.
- Contact: www.hopeandfreedom.com, www.hopeandfreedom.net

Inpatient Sex Addiction Treatment Centers

- Del Amo Hospital: Torrance, CA, www.delamoshospital.com
- Gentle Path at Pine Grove: Hattiesburg, MS, www.pinegrovetreatment.com
- Keystone Center: Chester, PA, www.keystonecenterecu.net

- Life Healing Center: Santa Fe, NM, www.life-healing.com
- The Meadows: Wickenburg, AZ, www.themeadows.org
- Sante Center for Healing: Argyle, TX, www.santecenter.com
- Sierra Tucson, Inc.: Tucson, AZ, www.sierratucson.com

Websites for Therapists Who Specialize in Sex Addiction

- The International Institute for Trauma and Addiction Professionals: www.iitap.com
- The Society for the Advancement of Sexual Healing: www.sash.net

Christian-Based Workshops

- Bethesda Workshops: Nashville, TN, www.bethesdaworkshops.org
- Be-Broken Ministries: Garden Ridge, TX, www.bebroken.com
- Faithful & True Ministries: Eden Prairie, MN, www.faithfulandtrue.com
- Journey of Hope Men's Retreats

Sex Addiction Recovery Websites

- www.journeytohealingandjoy.com
- www.celebritysexaddict.com
- www.gottostopit.com

- www.guardyoureyes.com
- www.hopeandfreedom.com
- www.hopeandfreedom.net
- www.hopeandfreedomu.com
- www.internetbehavior.com
- www.physiciansincrisis.com
- www.ldshopeandrecovery.com
- www.recoveryapp.com
- www.recoveryonthego.com
- www.saatalk.org
- www.sexhelp.com
- www.woundedclergy.com

12-Step Programs for Other Behaviors/Addictions

- Alcoholics Anonymous: www.aa.org
- Cocaine Anonymous: www.ca.org
- Crystal Meth Anonymous: www.crystal-meth.org
- Debtors Anonymous: www.debtorsanony-mous.org
- Food Addicts Anonymous: www.foodaddict-sanonymous.org
- Gamblers Anonymous: www.gamblersanon-ymous.org
- Marijuana Anonymous: www.marijua-na-anonymous.org
- Narcotics Anonymous: www.nicotine-anon-ymous.org
- Overeaters Anonymous: www.oa.org

- Spenders Anonymous: www.spenders.org
- Shopaholics Anonymous: www.shopaholic-sanonymous.org
- Workaholics Anonymous: www.workahol-ics-anonymous.org

iRecovery Addiction Recovery Tracker

- Assigns recovery points to typical recovery activities
- Charts those activities and compares progress from week to week
- Users can add their activities and assign a point value for each
- Will send weekly accountability emails to Circle of Five and therapist
- "Call Sponsor" button visible on every screen for immediate contact with sponsor
- Preloaded affirmations with counter
- Users can also add their own affirmations
- User-defined Red Light, Yellow Light, and Green l ight behaviors
- Contacts button takes users to list of their Circle of Five contacts
- Recovery points can be customized
- Contact: www.recoveryapp.com

ENDNOTES

History of the 12 Steps

1. Helen Thompson. "Meet the Doctor Who Convinced America to Sober Up." Smithsonian Magazine (July 6, 2015). Retrieved from www.smithsonianmagazine.smart-news/meet-the-doctor.

2. "The Birth of A.A. and Its Growth in the U.S." Alcoholics Anonymous. Retrieved from www.aa.org.

Chapter 1

1. John Calvin. "Commentary on Mark 5:9." Calvin's Commentary on the Bible. (Ada, MI: Baker Books, 2009). Retrieved from www.studylight.org/commentaries/cal/mark-1.html.

2. Jamie Arpin-Ricci. "Preach the Gospel at All Times." HuffPost (July 1, 2012).

3. C.S. Lewis. Mere Christianity. (New York: MacMillan, 1960). Retrieved from www.essentialcslewis.com.

Chapter 2

1. Charles Spurgeon. Spurgeon's Sermons, Volume 33. (London: Passmore & Alabaster, 1887). Retrieved from www.ccel.org.sermons33.liv.html.

2. Israel Drazin. "There Are Not 613 Biblical Commands." (May 31, 2017). Retrieved from www.blogs.timesofisrael.com.

Chapter 3

1. James Ross Kelly. "The Story of the Loving Father—William Barclay." (September 5, 2014). Retrieved from www.stjohnoneone.com.

2. Louis Bertrand. St. Augustin. (New York: D. Appleton & Co., 1914). Retrieved from www.fulltextarchive.com.

3. Vance Havner. Retrieved from www.brainyquote.com/quotes/vance.havner_152358.

4. St. Augustine. "Going Back to See the Elephants." Confessions, Book 8, Chapter 20. (New York: Image Books, 1960), 185.

5. Tony Robbins. Retrieved from www.brainyquote.com/quotes/tony_robbins?147787.

6. John C. Maxwell. Motivated to Succeed. (Nashville, TN: Thomas Nelson Publishers, 2006), 23.

7. The Number 23. Directed by Joel Schumacher. (Contrafilm, 2007).

8. Henri Nouwen. The Return of the Prodigal Son. (New York: Random House, 1992), 17.

9. Joseph Sunde. "Homesick at Home: Chesterton on the Paradox of Exile." (February 2, 2016). Retrieved from www.letterstotheexiles.com.

Chapter 4

1. Sandro Boricelli. "Hearts Are Restless." Retrieved from www.christianhistoryinstitute.org.

2. Alcoholics Anonymous, Fourth Edition. (Alcoholics Anonymous World Services, Inc., 2002), 45.

3. Bryant McGill. "One of the Most Sincere Forms of respect." USA Today, September 4, 2018.

4. Chris Tomlin. "Jesus My Redeemer." (Brentwood, TN: Capitol Christian Music Group, And If God Is For Us, 2010).

5. Clarence Snyder. Going Through the Steps. (Alcoholics Anonymous World Services, Inc., 1944). Retrieved from www.a-1associates.com/clarencesnyder.

6. Lauren Fox. "The Science of Cohabitation." The Atlantic. (March 20, 2014).

7. John Piper. "The Tragic Cost of Her Cavernous Thirst." (June 21, 2009). Retrieved from www.desiringgod.messages.the-tragic-cost-of-her-cavernous-thirst.

Chapter 5

1. Stephen Arterburn. The Secrets Men Keep. (Nashville, TN: Thomas Nelson, 2006).

2. Alcoholics Anonymous, 57.

3. Patrick Carnes. Facing the Shadows. (Wickenburg, AZ: Gentle Path Press, 2000). Retrieved from www.strengtheningmarriage.com/facing-the-shadows.

Chapter 6

1. Alcoholics Anonymous, 63.

2. Jon Bloom. "The Merciful Gift of Desperation." (February 6, 2014). Retrieved from www.desiringgod.com/articles.the-merciful-gift-of-desperation.

3. Martin Lloyd-Jones. "D. Martyn Lloyd-Jones Quotes." Retrieved from www.goodreads.com.

4. Kevin Halloran. "D.L. Moody Quotes: Inspiring Quotations by Dwight L. Moody." (February 5, 2013). Retrieved from www.kevinhalloran.net.

5. Tim Keller. Twitter. (March 14, 2014). Retrieved from twitter.com/timkellernyc/status/44503440941907698?lang=en.

6. Andrew Murray. Retrieved from www.christianvideotv.com.

Chapter 7

1. Robert Hemfelt. Serenity: A Companion for Twelve Step Recovery. (Nashville, TN: Thomas Nelson, 1990), 54-55.

2. Alcoholics Anonymous, 76.

3. Rick Warren. The Purpose Driven Life. (Grand Rapids, MI: Zondervan, 2002), Day 19.

4. Billy Graham. "Prayer 101: How Do I Talk to God?" Retrieved from www.billygraham.org.

5. Charles Spurgeon. Spurgeon's Sermons, Volume 17. (London: Passmore & Alabaster Publishing, 1871). Retrieved from www.ccel.org.spurgeon.

6. Kevin Kruse. "Zig Ziglar: 10 Quotes that Can Change Your Life." (November 28, 2012). Retrieved from www.forbes.com.

7. John Bunyan. Pilgrim's Progress. Posted by Deen Carnes. (October 12, 2015). Retrieved from www.reformedspirit.blogspot.com.

8. Bob Smietana. "Lifeway Study." Christianity Today. (August 15, 2017).

Chapter 8

1. August Wilson. "August Wilson Quotes, from Successories." Retrieved from www.successories.com.

2. Rick Warren. "12 Inspirational Rick Warren Quotes on Forgiveness." The Christian Post. Retrieved from www.post.christianpost.com/post/12-inspirationalrickwarrenquotes.

3. Laura Moncur. "Laura Moncur's Motivational Quotations." (Quotation #31674). Retrieved from www.quotationspage.com.

Chapter 9

1. Joe McQ. The Steps We Took. (Atlanta, GA: August House Publishing, 1990), 119.

2. Craig Cashwell. Shadows of the Cross. (Carefree, AZ: Gentle Path Press, 2015), 76.

3. Mark Laaser. Healing the Wounds of Sexual Addiction. (Grand Rapids, MI: Zondervan, 2004), 123.

4. Tim Stoddart. Sober Nation. "The Difference Between Making Amends and Making Apologies." Sober Nation. (July 12, 2014). Retrieved from www.sobernation.com/makingamends.com.

5. Bill W. Twelve Steps and Twelve Traditions. (Alcoholics Anonymous Publ. Co., 1952), 83.

6. Tamar Chansky. Freeing Yourself from Anxiety. (Boston, MA: Da Capo Lifelong Books, 2012). Retrieved from www.tamarchansky.com.

7. Alcoholics Anonymous, 85.

8. Michael McCullough. "Holding a Grudge Produces Cortisol and Diminishes Oxytocin." Psychology Today. (April 11, 2015). Retrieved from www.psychologytoday.intl.blog.

9. Jennifer Matesa. "Sexual Amends in Addiction Recovery." Hazelden Betty Ford Foundation. (September 20, 2016). Retrieved from www.hazeldon.bettyford.matesa.sexualamendsinaddictionrecovery.com.

Chapter 10

1. Jennifer Porter. "Why You Should Make Time for Self." Harvard Business Review. (March 21, 2017). Retrieved from www.hbr.org.

2. Amy Klobuchar. Retrieved from www.brainy-quote.com.

3. Milton Magness and Marsha Means. Real Hope, True Freedom. (Las Vegas, NV: Central Recovery Press, 2017), 89.

4. Harry Kraemer. "How Self-Reflection Can Make You a Better Leader." (December 2, 2016). Retrieved from www.insight.kellogg.northwestern.edu.

5. JM Olejarz. "Three Components of an Inventory." Harvard Business Review. (November, 2015). Retrieved from www.harvardbusinessreview.com.

6. Douglass Eury. "5 Quick Steps of Reflective Practice," based on Rethink, Rebuild, Rebound. (2011). Retrieved from www.teachhub.com.

7. Juli Slattery. Rethinking Sexuality. (New York: Multnomah Publishing, 2018), 35.

Chapter 11

1. Bill W. My First 40 Years. (Center City, MN: Hazelden Publishing, 2005), 145.

2. St. Augustine. Retrieved from www.olmlay-carmelites.org.

3. Gabor Mate. Interview, 2017. Retrieved from www.upliftconnect.com.

4. Frank McAndrew. "The Perils of Social Isolation." Psychology Today. (November 12, 2016).

5. Ralph Waldo Emerson. (Posted May 27, 2014). Retrieved from www.quoteinvestigator.com.

6. Blaise Pascal. "The Misery of Man Without God." Harvard Classics. (1909). Retrieved from www.bartleby.com.

7. William Lane Craig. "Wise Men Still Seek Him." American Association of Christian Counselors. (December 17, 2016). Retrieved from www.aacc.net.

8. Rick Warren. Twitter. (December 12, 2014). Retrieved from www.quotefancy.com.rickwarren.the-most-common-mistake.

Chapter 12

1. Neil Diamond. "Brother Love's Travelling Salvation Show." (Santa Monica, CA: Universal Music Group, 1969.)

2. Alcoholics Anonymous, 106.

3. St. Augustine. Retrieved from www.brainy-quotes.saint.augustine.com.

4. Eusebius. The History of the Church. (Oxford: Clarendon Press, 1834). Retrieved from www.en.m.wikepedia.org.

5. Nestor the Chronicler. (Chronicle of Nestor, circa 1100). Retrieved from www.faithworks.life.who-was-st-andrew.com.

6. William Barclay. Daily Study Bible. (Louisville, KY: Westminster John Knox Press, 1978). Retrieved from www.studylight.org.

7. Ronald Reagan. "A Time for Choosing." (Speech, October 27, 1964). Retrieved from www.reaganlibrary.gov.

8. Carol Burnett. Retrieved from www.brainy-quotes.carol.burnett.371198.

9. B.P. Dore. "Personality and Social Psychology Bulletin." Columbia University Study, 2017. Retrieved from www.psycnet.apa.org.

10. Step into Action. (SAICO, 2004), 185.

11. Marianna Pogosyan. "In Helping Others, You Help Yourself." Psychology Today. (May 30, 2018).

12. Sarah Arpin, presenter. Society for Personality and Social Psychology Annual Convention. (January 21, 2017). Retrieved from www.cossa.org.event.2017.com.

13. Craig Impelman. "Wooden's 7-Point Creed." (January 18, 2017). Retrieved from www.thewooden-effect.com.

Conclusion

1. Conor Bezane. Blog, "Sober Heroes—Betty Ford." (July 19, 2018). Retrieved from www.conorbezane.com/soberheroes-betty-ford.

Appendix A

1. Mark Denison. Porn in the Pew. (Fort Worth, TX: Austin Brothers, 2018), 16-20.

Appendix J

1. Tori Rodriguez. "Criticism of 12-Step Groups: Is It Warranted?" (October 5, 2016). Retrieved from www.psychiatryadvisor.com.

2. Ibid.

3. Ibid.

4. David Sack, "Why the Hostility Toward the 12 Steps?" (October 20, 2012). Retrieved from www.psychologytoday.com.

5. Tori Rodriguez, "Criticism of 12-Step Groups: Is It Warranted?"

ABOUT
THERE'S STILL HOPE

After a 30-year career as a senior pastor, Mark and Beth Denison launched *There's Still Hope* to bring recovery and restoration to those who suffer from porn and sex addiction, and their spouses. Ministering out of their personal history with sex addiction, and having completed extensive training in the field, Mark and Beth offer several programs and resources for those in need. These include the following:

- 90-day recovery program for sex addicts
- One-year maintenance program for addicts
- Personal coaching for spouses
- 12-week group for spouses
- One-day intensives for couples
- Specialized groups for pastors
- Recovery Minute—a daily email devotion
- Presentations for churches, colleges, and high schools
- Conference presentations

While pastoring three churches in Texas over 30 years, Mark also served as Board Chair at Houston

Baptist University three times, and was a chaplain for the Houston Rockets for five seasons. His education includes four degrees: B.A. (HBU), M.A.H.S. in Addiction (Liberty University), as well as an M.Div. and D.Min. from Southwestern Baptist Theological Seminary. Mark has also been trained and certified as a Pastoral Sex Addiction Professional (PSAP) and is an active member of the American Association of Christian Counselors (AACC).

Beth was a popular speaker at ladies events while serving the churches Mark pastored in Texas. She did her undergraduate work at HBU and is a Certified Life Coach (CLC) and Partner Recovery Coach (PRC). Married in 1983, the Denisons live near their son and daughter-in-law just ten minutes from the beautiful beaches of Bradenton, Florida, where they are active leaders in their local church.

Other Books Written by Mark and Beth

Porn in the Pew
365 Days to Sexual Integrity
A 90-Day Guide to Recovery
Porn-Free in 40 Days
Daily Walk
12-Week Spouse Recovery Guide

www.ingramcontent.com/pod-product-compliance
Lightning Source LLC
Chambersburg PA
CBHW060012100426
42740CB00010B/1468